Mystic Science
VASTU

Explore Vastushastra in the new Millennium. For a long time debate has been going on whether to treat Vastushastra as a science, a statistical statement, metaphysics, or some occult practice. To prove anything conclusively one needs to use all the tools at hand - science, mathematics, logic, Yogashastra, astrology, Ayurveda, etc. It must be understood that modern science, as we know it has developed in the Western world over the last 300 years, cannot be used as the only yardstick for judging the science of Vastu which evolved some 5000 years ago in India. Science has its own importance in its search for truth and for its logical view of events. Current educational practices give all the credit to Western science and dismiss ancient Indian science and Eastern philosophy as occult disciplines and mysticism. We have to break this narrow-minded conditioned thinking process and study Vastushastra with an open mind to demystify its occult garb.

In this book, the authors have stressed the importance of *Darshanshastra* in Vastushastra studies, since Vastushastra, Yogashastra, astrology, Ayurveda, and Sangeet are sub-branches of *Darshanshastra*. Learning of Vastushastra becomes simple and interesting with parallel concepts from Yogashastra, astrology, science, and Vastushastra being presented throughout the book. One can have a broader perspective of Vastushastra only through a multi-disciplinary approach, as illustrated in the book.

By the same authors

SECRETS OF VASTUSHASTRA
ISBN 81 207 2042 3, pp. 128, Rs 100

Published by
Sterling Publishers Private Limited

Mystic Science of
VASTU

N.H. SAHASRABUDHE
M.E. (I.I.Sc), Vastu Vachaspati

R.D. MAHATME
M.Tech

New Dawn

NEW DAWN
a division of Sterling Publishers (P) Ltd.
L-10, Green Park Extension, New Delhi-110016
Ph.: 6191784, 6191785, 6191023 Fax: 91-11-6190028
E-mail: ghai@nde.vsnl.net.in
Internet: http://www.sterlingpublishers.com

Mystic Science of Vastu
©2000, N.H. Sahasrabudhe & R.D. Mahatme
ISBN 81 207 2206 x

All rights are reserved. No part of this publication may be reproduced, stored in a retrieval system or transmitted, in any form or by any means, mechanical, photocopying, recording or otherwise, without prior written permission of the publisher.

Published by Sterling Publishers Pvt. Ltd., New Delhi-110016.
Lasertypeset by Vikas Compographics, New Delhi-110029.
Printed at Ram Printograph (India),

With love and respect we dedicate this book to

Guruji Sri Sri Ravishankar

*Founder,
Art of Living Foundation
&
Ved Vidnyan Maha Vidyapeeth
whose divine presence inspires and guides us in life*

PREFACE

Darshanshastra is the starting point for understanding the significance of any of the ancient Indian sciences. The extensively studied disciplines like *Yogashastra*, *Jyotishshastra*, *Vastushastra*, *Ayurved*, and *Sangeet* have their origins in *Darshanshastra*. Rather, these disciplines are known as '*Upangas*' (sub-branches) of *Darshanshastra*.

It is interesting to note that all these sub-branches follow a common logical pattern for analysing and understanding a given situation. Astrology studies the effect of planetary positions and directions on an individual, while *Vastushastra* studies the impact on a *Vastu*, of cosmic energy and cosmic forces with all their directional aspects. In all these disciplines, a *Vastu* is assumed to be a living soul having close affinity with the individual dwelling in it.

Vastushastra - Theory & Practice

Life, though beyond logic, is certainly not illogical. Life descends from immensity that is an ocean of logic. But, this immensity itself is infinitely so far away from man's comprehension that it makes him wonder whether the life itself is beyond logic.

Minute microscopic human thoughts cannot find cosmic link. Holistic existence can create contradictions with logic, the all-purpose source of life. Traditional sciences reflect this fundamental truth through the comprehensive perception of nature. Perception begins where the confines of cause and effect end. Traditional medical disciplines lead to *Kaya Kalpa* (transformation of body), *Yogashastra* results in *Mana Kalpa* (transformation of mind), and *Vastushastra* shows the way to *Bhagya Kalpa* (transformation of fortunes).

Water, wind, light, stones, metals, plants, herbs, pyramids, crystals, colours, helix, mystic curves serve as catalysts in *Vastushastra* for rectifying the cosmic alignment of an individual. Changes brought about in the holistic existence of man by these remedial measures guide him to positive relationships, satisfaction in all his endeavours, happiness, bliss, and grace.

Enhancing the benign moon-streams (*Ida*) and curtailing the devastating sun-streams (*Pingala*) are the foundations of *Vastushastra*. The core *Vastushastra* revolves round addition, subtraction, manipulation, and reworking of virtues and vices of *Panch-Maha-Bhutas* (five great elements) projected through human beings and nature. The divine knowledge of *Vastu* can provide cosmic envelope to human beings at all levels of existence.

Jyotisha (astrology) and *Yogashastra* are prerequisites for learning *Vastushastra*. Cosmos is divided into 27 parts known as constellations. These constellations are classified on the basis of five great elements and planets. The virtues and vices of five great elements are reflected in certain earthly entities like plants, colours, metals, and gems that are under the influence of constellations. The relationship of directions with plants, colours, metals, stones gives great variety and multiple dimensions to *Vastu* remedial measures. A new momentum is imparted to cosmic rhythm, directional frequencies, and natural synchronies through these corrective actions. An individual is then freed of his old reference and exposed to fresh reality. *Vastushastra* blesses him with a new direction in life, fresh span, and a unique axis of reference.

Yogashastra deals with inner spaces of human beings. Spaces with *Satwa Guna* are full of *Prana*, spaces with *Rajo Guna* are filled with essayed self-ego, and spaces with *Tamo Guna* are nothing but voids in life. Yogic processes refill all these spaces with *Prana* and transform all the voids in the macrocosm of primordial sounds. *Vastushastra* in coordination with astrology and *Yogashastra* can provide a holistic curve for all the problems in the world.

While constructing a house, the divine *Vastu* knowledge reflects the qualities of an individual and the cosmos, as *Vastushastra* is the cosmic bridge between microcosm, the inner spaces and macrocosm, the outer spaces.

Vibrations, waves, sound, and light are the four basic instruments of *Vastushastra*. Examples are aplenty to indicate that

Preface

a right blending of these parameters leads to positivity, while a wrong combination leads to negativity.

For ages, astrology has been used for understanding and predicting an individual's destiny. Astrology has also been extensively referred to for pinpointing the state of mind and body of a person, including any diseases, afflictions and handicaps. Since *Vastushastra* treats any *Vastu* as a living soul, it is not difficult to understand the relevance of astrology to gain insight into the physical state of a *Vastu*. The starting point for astrology is defining the positions of planets in specific directions, while *Vastushastra* analysis has *Vastu*-directions as the operating factor. Thus a common platform for both these disciplines is easily established.

After an extensive study of hundreds of dwellings, horoscopes of the owners of these houses, their living conditions, their careers, their family backgrounds, etc., it was evident that the horoscopes of the occupants of the *Vastu* could pinpoint the *Vastu-dosha* of their dwellings. Deciding the effective remedial measures against *Vastu-dosha* on the basis of the horoscope and the *Vastu-Purush-Mandal* was the next logical step. During this exercise, it became abundantly clear that the matching of astrology and *Vastushastra* was flawless, whether it was *Vastu*-situation or the remedial measures.

While *Jyotisha* gives insight into *Vastu-dosha* and general remedial action, *Yogashastra* shows the path towards building a protective shield against effects of directional deficiencies. Modern science can serve its purpose in providing an analytical approach and efficient techniques in implementing *Vastu* principles. *Vastushastra* inquiry must involve a multidisciplinary and multidimensional approach for providing succour to the human mind that has lost its way in the confusing scenario of the modern era.

N.H. Sahasrabudhe
R.D. Mahatme

CONTENTS

Preface   v

1. **Vastu Purush Mandal**   1
   1.1 Theoretical Perception as Reflected in Modern Science
   1.2 Jaivik Urja and Pranik Urja
   1.3 Consciousness

2. **Forces, Fields, and Vastu**   7
   2.1 Solar Radiation and Vastu
   2.2 Hartmann's Grid
   2.3 Source and Sink Directions, and Vastu

3. **Cosmic Energy and Vastu**   14
   3.1 Energy Dynamics
   3.2 Inverted Volcano of Cosmic Energy
   3.3 Vortex of Energy Imbalance
   3.4 Cyclic Helix of Matter Balance
   3.5 Energy Forms - Multidisciplinary Approach

4. **Yogashastra Concepts in Vastu Science**   23
   4.1 Yogashastra and Vastushastra
   4.2 Vastu Nabhi
   4.3 Ida, Pingala, and Directions
   4.4 Insight into Yoga-Vastu
   4.5 Yogashastra - Path to Contentment

5. **Vastu-dosha and Yogic Remedies**   35
   5.1 Arghyadan (अर्घ्यदान)
   5.2 Homa-Havan - (होम हवन) The Fire Worship
   5.3 Sudarshan Kriya (सुदर्शन क्रिया)
   5.4 Shaktipat Yoga Diksha and Reiki
   5.5 Transcendental Meditation
   5.6 Pranayama and Yogasana
   5.7 Vipasana
   5.8 Soham Sadhana

6. **Astrology in Vastu Analysis**   45
    6.1 Astrology and Vastushastra
    6.2 Horoscope and Vastu-dosha
    6.3 Vastu-dosha and Cyclic Repetition
    6.4 Analytical Case

7. **Vastu-Jyotisha**   59
    7.1 Vastu-Jyotisha Case Studies
    7.2 Chandranadi, Suryanadi, and Vastu-Jyotisha

8. **Vastu-dosha and Remedial Action**   67
    8.1 Vastu-dosha Analysis through Vastu-Jyotisha
    8.2 Directions, Planets, and Vastushastra
    8.3 Chanting of Mantra
    8.4 Application of Yantra
    8.5 Precious Stones, Pearls, and Jewels
    8.6 Colours
    8.7 Cosmic Baths

9. **Tantra, Mantra, and Yoga in Vastu Science**   76
    9.1 Purva-Sanskara, Prarabdha, Jyotisha, and Vastukundli
    9.2 Laws of Nature and Vastu Rules
    9.3 Tantra
    9.4 Mantra
    9.5 Vastu Yantra
    9.6 Practical Vastu Remedies

10. **Energy Concept in Temple Architecture**   99
    10.1 Vastu Aspect of Some Religious Places

11. **Architecture Today - a Vastu View**   107
    11.1 Vastushastra and Modern Architecture
    11.2 Vastu Architecture

12. **Industrial Structures**   113
    12.1 North Light Structures
    12.2 North-South Length
    12.3 Work Environment for Executives and Staff
    12.4 Zoning of Industrial Activities
    12.5 Landscaping and Loads
    12.6 The Helix
    12.7 Vastu Analysis for an Industrial Unit

13. Vastu in Practice   123
    13.1 Office Site
    13.2 Warehousing Complex
    13.3 Office Building
    13.4 Geographical Site

14. Nature, Macroworld, and Vastushastra Rules   131
    14.1 Past and Future 50 Years for India

15. Vastushastra and Event Manifest   138
    15.1 Astrology in Vastu Prognosis
    15.2 Vastushastra and Statistical Forecast

16. Glimpses of Traditional Vastushastra   144
    16.1 Methods of Vastu Classification
    16.2 Aura of Two Streams and Concept of Marma-Sthan
    16.3 Selection of Soil Characteristics
    16.4 Intellectual Classes, Military and Police, Traders and Businessmen, Working Classes
    16.5 Comments
    16.6 Prangan Pravesh

17. Vastushastra Guidelines   160
    17.1 Before Planning a Vastu
    17.2 Vastu-kshetra Analysis through Vastu-Jyotisha
    17.3 Vithi-Shula
    17.4 Vastu Rules for Agriculture

    Conclusion   176

INDEX OF FIGURES, CHARTS, TABLES, AND PLATES

Figures

1.1	Darshanshastra and Sub-branches
1.2	Deities for Eight Directions in Vastu Purush Mandal
2.1	Vastu Subjected to Thermal Radiation from Solar Flux
2.2	Energy Source and Sink Directions for a Vastu
2.3	Zones of Influence for Directions
2.4	Flooring Pattern Based on Vastu Purush Mandal & Qualities of Five Great Elements
3.1	Relative Thermal Activity of Different Zones
3.2	Relative Matter Density for Different Directions
7.1	Horoscope for Analytical Case (I)
7.2	Horoscope for Analytical Case (II)
7.3	Horoscope for Analytical Case (III)
7.4	Horoscope for Analytical Case (IV)
7.5	Building Height versus Relative Intensity of Ill-effects due to Flaws in Moon-streams and Sun-streams
7.6	Directionwise Zoning of Row-Housing Complex
8.1	Directions and Ruling Planets
12.1	Sketch and Landscape Details of Industrial Plot
12.2	Schematic of Internal Changes as per Vastu Tenets
14.1	Directions and Planetary Considerations in Vastu-Jyotisha of India
15.1	Vastu Purush Mandal
16.1	Chatushashtipad Vastu Matrix
16.2	Ekshitipad Vastu Matrix
16.3	Shatpad Vastu Matrix
16.4	Marmasthan in Vastu Purush Mandal
16.5a	Habitation Zone for Intellectuals

16.5b Habitation Zone for Military/Police
16.5c Habitation Zone for Traders
16.5d Habitation for Working Classes
16.6 Slopes and Gradients
16.7 Dwar Nivesh Phal
17.1 Horoscopic Projection
17.2 Shape of a Plot and Astrological Significance (I)
17.3 Shape of a Plot and Astrological Significance (II)
17.4 Shape of a Plot and Astrological Significance (III)
17.5 Shape of a Plot and Astrological Significance (IV)
17.6 Vithi-Shula (I)
17.7 Vithi-Shula (II)
17.8. Planning of Rooms in a Household as per Vastu Principles
17.9 Industrial Layout as per Vastushastra

Tables

Chart 6.1 Generic Names of Trees in Avak-Hada-Chakra
Chart 9.1 Akshar Varnamala and Panch-Maha-Bhutas
Table 4.1 Characteristics of Panch-Maha-Bhutas
4.2 Elements of Vedic Origin in Vastushastra Concepts
4.3 Correlation between Great Elements and Energy Forms in Vedic Scriptures
4.4 Vastushastra Equation with Yogashastra, Astrology, and Science
5.1 Preferred Rituals for Specific Directions
6.1 Constellations, Great Elements, and Benevolent Trees
6.2 Qualities of Five Great Elements
6.3 Lord Planets - Zodiac Signs - Five Great Elements
6.4 Directions and Planets in Astrology
6.5 Astrological Relationship between Planets
8.1 Precious Stones and Metals for Garnering Positive Planetary Energies
8.2 Choice of Colours Based on Owner's Zodiac Sign
8.3 Colour scheme Based on Directions and Planets

8.4 Shri Ranga Chakra
8.5 Plants and Herbs for Use in Ritualistic Bath
14.1 Planetary Twelve Year Cycle and India
15.1 Significance of Various Houses in a Horoscope
16.1 Applications of Shatpad Vastu, Ekshitipad Vastu, and Chatushashtipad Vastu
16.2 Land Characteristics and Personal Fortunes

Plates

Plate 1 Ishanya Yantra
Plate 2 Pyramids
Plate 3 Urdhwa Gurutwa Yantra
Plate 4 Nairutya Pushkarini (Sketch)
Plate 5 Dakshin Tamra Samvahak and Bhoumya Yantra
Plate 6 Mirrors
Plate 7 Lunar Shaped Water Surface in Northeast Direction
Plate 8 Wooden Pyramidal Ceiling
Plate 9 Pyramids over Southern Entrance
Plate 10 Glass Bricks
Plate 11 Stone Pillar in Southwest Direction
Plate 12 Schematic Sketch of Hazratbal Shrine in Kashmir
Plate 13 Synagogue Lal Deval in Pune
Plate 14 North-South Virtue Enhancement through Cylindrical Shell Ceiling
Plate 15 Lead Disc with Blue Crystals for West Wall
Plate 16 Bhoumya Yantra and Copper Conducting Plates for the South Wall
Plate 17 Plan Modified as per Vastu for Warehousing Complex
Plate 18 Plan as per Vastu for the Office Complex
Plate 19 Geographical Layout of the Site

1. VASTU PURUSH MANDAL

1.1 Theoretical Perception as Reflected in Modern Science

Darshanshastra is an outcome of comprehensive perception of Nature. A logical statement, in general, cannot cope up with totality of a situation, but perception never ever fails to register reality in its true perspective. Comprehensive perception is the expression of reality resulting from oneness of the observer, the observed, and the observation. As a subject matter, and as an outcome of human endeavour for seeking truth, perception comprehensively outperforms the much-discussed "Cause and Effect" theory. Ancient texts term the pattern of perception as **bliss**, as it has blossomed out of human culture after doing away with constraints like stereotypes and patterns in all walks of life. Perception is not a manoeuvring by a clever mind, but rather an expression of order of Nature.

Darshanshastra explains and narrates the state of human existence as a single stream of consciousness, termed as *Sat Chit Anand*. It must be remembered that the term *Sat Chit Anand* cannot be equated with meaning associated with the word 'freedom', which follows as a corollary from the term 'bondage'. *Sat Chit Anand* implies free spirit beyond any boundaries of space and time.

The five sub-branches (*Upangas*) of *Darshanshastra* are basically applied engineering sciences, which have formulated the comprehensive perception in terms of energy-matter, cause-effect etc. Each of the five *Upangas* derives its structure from specific conceptual elements. The *Upangas* and the source elements are tabulated below. Anybody interested in Indian cultural ethos is generally conversant with the *Upangas* - Music, Astrology, Medicine, *Yogashastra* and *Vastushastra* - albeit as separate disciplines. Since these sciences are studied as specialised topics, people sometimes fail to notice the *Darshanshastra* origin of these fields.

These five sub-branches of *Darshanshastra* are associated with various energy forms necessary for commencement, preservation, development and evolution of life. The *Upangas* play important role in preparing fertile ground for seed of life to flower and eternally experience the *Sat Chit Anand*. Traditionally this is known as "*Kshema of Yoga*", the eternal euphoria.

Darshanshastra
|
Upanga (Sub-branch)

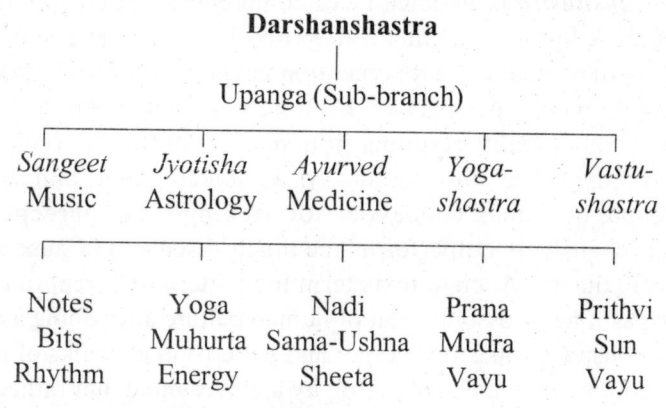

Sangeet	*Jyotisha*	*Ayurved*	*Yoga-*	*Vastu-*
Music	Astrology	Medicine	*shastra*	*shastra*
Notes	Yoga	Nadi	Prana	Prithvi
Bits	Muhurta	Sama-Ushna	Mudra	Sun
Rhythm	Energy	Sheeta	Vayu	Vayu

Fig.1.1: Darshanshastra and its sub-branches

We are discussing here the link between Modern Science and *Vastu-Purush-Mandal*. By identifying the significance of deities associated with definite directions in a *Vastu-Purush-Mandal* in terms of modern science, we will try to find the hidden causality relationship. It will then be easy to see how the perception in this traditional science matches with logic and results of modern science.

In all *Vedic* literature, symbols and similes are used as a metaphor for explaining facts and procedures. These symbols are basically 'the perfect one word expression' for the process involved. Over a period of time we have lost the meanings of these symbols and in the present era, a stranglehold of objective methods of modern science has resulted in a certain degree of ambiguity in approach to these ancient sciences. It has now become extremely important to breach this silence of tradition and the vague response of modern science.

Here, we will try to delineate the traditional narration in terms of the basic laws, logic and approach of quantum mechanics, particle physics, biochemistry and energy dynamics. For correlating the significance of Goddesses, directions, and forces in *Vastu-Purush-Mandal* the following topics are very significant - flow characteristics of solar energy, geomagnetic flux, thermal variations disturbing the electromagnetic flux lines, vector analysis of two important energy fields relative to position of the sun, sub-atomic particles, thought and consciousness as energy fields, waves and vibrations.

There are two important ideas in understanding the relevance of solar energy and geomagnetic energy for a *Vastu*. The first concept is based on vector analysis of the ever-changing directional solar energy field as imposed on steady North-South geomagnetic flux. The second concept tries to understand the relationship between electromagnetic flux and movement of sub-atomic particles.

1.2 Jaivik Urja and Pranik Urja

The north-south geomagnetic flux is termed as जैविक उर्जा (*Jaivik Urja* i.e. organic energy) in ancient Indian texts. This force field helps in locating the energy medians in living beings and providing them with natural orientation. This eternal unidirectional flow defines, directs and propagates the existence at cellular level. The solar energy flux keeps on changing as per the position of the sun relative to the earth. This force field with photon quanta as energy packets is classically termed as प्राणिक उर्जा (*Pranik Urja*).

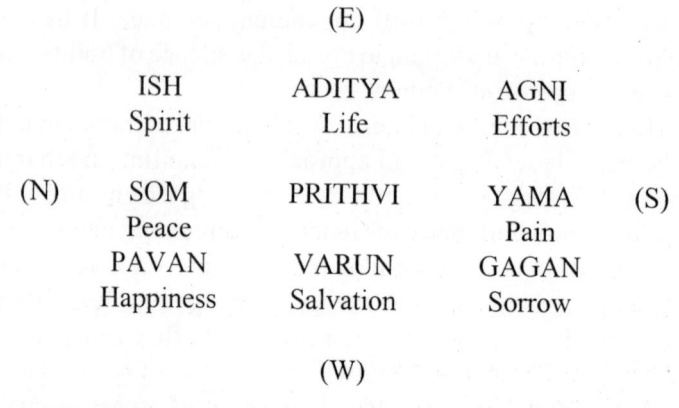

```
                        (E)

        ISH         ADITYA        AGNI
        Spirit      Life          Efforts

(N)     SOM         PRITHVI       YAMA     (S)
        Peace                     Pain

        PAVAN       VARUN         GAGAN
        Happiness   Salvation     Sorrow

                        (W)
```

Fig.1.2: Deities for Eight Directions in Vastu-Purush-Mandal

In *Vastu-Purush-Mandal*, deities are identified with the positive or negative confluence of these fluxes in relation to changing position of the sun. The symbolic nomenclatures, the deities, their spheres of influence as related to virtues and vices are self-explanatory.

The positive confluence is termed as प्रीति संगम (*Preeti-Sangam*), implying that two streams have merged into one, and are flowing forward to reinforce the dynamic characteristic of each flow in the direction of propagation. During the night, the sun is in the North zone with respect to the earth, creating the right conditions for *Preeti-Sangam*. In *Vastu-Purush-Mandal*, the deities associated with the North zone - *Pavan*, *Som*, and *Ish* - represent all the bliss and contentment in Nature.

Pranik Urja or solar flux represents dynamic ever-changing vector field that moves through 360 degrees in relation to the earth while the flow of *Jaivik Urja* is unidirectional in ever-fixed North-South vector field. Wherever friendship, unification or reinforcement of *Jaivik Urja* and *Pranik Urja* take shape, life finds heavenly bliss. Oneness of *Prana* and *Jeeva* is termed as life. There lies the significance of *Pavan*, *Som*, and *Ish* being identified as deities of the North zone.

During the day, the sun traverses the East, Southeast, South, Southwest and West path. Even in the '*Uttarayan*' (winter solstice), there is a maximum of 10-degree variation, implying thereby that solar flux is almost constant throughout the year.

The Southeast and Southwest zones receive the maximum solar energy in its full intensity. These are the zones where the solar energy field is in opposition to the natural geomagnetic flux. In other words, *Pranik Urja* and *Jaivik Urja* work against each other and are on inimical terms in these zones. Wherever there is antagonistic relationship between these forces, life is subjected to hardship, pain, and sorrow. *Jeeva* devoid of *Prana* is termed as death. In *Vastu-Purush-Mandal* this battlefield is defined through the three deities - *Agni, Yama,* and *Nairuti*. The nomenclatures are self-explanatory.

Mutually opposite flows of Pranik and Jaivik fluxes is termed as शिव-तांडव (*Shiv-Tandav*) i.e. demonic dance of Shiva. Reinforcement of these forces i.e. प्रीति संगम is known in mythological terms as चिद्-विलास (*Chid-Vilas*).

In vector analysis of these forces with respect to the earth's self-rotating motion, the Northeast represents उगम (*Ugam* i.e. source) of the unified energies and the diagonally opposite direction, the Southwest represents अंत (*Anta* i.e. sink) of all the energies. The vector that connects the Northeast point to the Southwest point, i.e. source to sink, is termed as the *Life Diagonal* or the *Energy Diagonal of the Vastu*. Vastu should be planned in such a way that the nabhi of the Vastu falls on lower one-third of this diagonal towards the Southwest direction.

1.3 Consciousness

In *Darshanshastra*, consciousness is known as तेजस् द्रव्यम् (Tejas Dravyam). Perception is defined here as the outcome of outward flow of mind and its interaction with external energy and matter. The positive or negative confluence of mind-energy or mind-matter is visualised as good or bad experience in inner spaces of the mind.

Quantum mechanics states that energy is available in quanta or specific energy packets only. Energy field can have positive or negative potential depending on the characteristics of the interacting matter. As far as processes taking place in biosphere are concerned, positive energy form is the one that motivates, propagates, enhances, and blesses life. Negative form is associated with processes that impede, destroy or annihilate life.

By providing insight into nature of these energy forms even at micro level, *Darshanshastra* and its sub-branches try to fortify life-sustaining positive energy forms. In understanding Nature, traditional means employing comprehensive perception have a definite edge over known modern scientific techniques.

Vastu-Purush-Mandal symbolically represents this amalgamation of good and bad in life and charts the path that can avoid vices and reinforce the virtuous qualities.

2. FORCES, FIELDS, AND VASTU

2.1 Solar Radiation and Vastu

It is observed that one side of a Vastu or a house is subjected to intense solar radiation, while the other side remains in shadow region. This leads to formation of औष्णिक द्वंद्व (*Aushnik Dwandwa*) or a thermocouple in the space around the house. In tropical countries, the Southeast, South, and Southwest directions suffer scorching sun, while the North, Northeast, and East directions are in cool shadow region (Fig. 2.1)

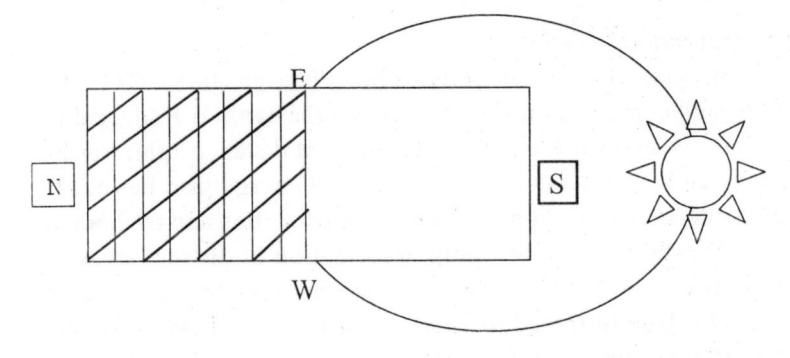

Fig. 2.1: Vastu subjected to thermal radiation from solar flux

We can surmise that higher imbalance creates disturbances in the naturally ordered geomagnetic flux lines, with formation of nodes at the points where flux lines cross each other. The nodes represent distorted energy potential and sub-atomic particles travelling along the flux lines can get trapped at such dislocations. Under specific conditions, these particles can start resonating to give off hazardous micro-level radiation. These emissions can work against the existence of life forms. *Vastu-Purush-Mandal* represents this phenomenon through the symbol '*Yama*' (death).

The thermal imbalance is the main cause in creating obstacles in smooth energy flow through and around the Vastu. The comprehensive remedial measures available in *Vastushastra* try to equalise the thermal differentials and provide harmonious and blissful living conditions for the dweller.

The disturbance in the South direction can be offset by the following measures;
1. Thick, heavy walls on the South side,
2. Blocking of openings on the South side,
3. Avoiding any slopes towards the South,
4. Orienting the house in such a manner that more open spaces are available in the North and East directions,
5. Planting of 'Audumber' trees in the South for availing of humid atmosphere,
6. Raising of plinth and compound height, in the South direction.

2.2 Hartmann's Grid

Dr. Hartmann has proposed that a bio-electromagnetic (B.E.M.) grid can be traced around the surface of the earth. B.E.M. grid in essence is a network of energy contours at distance 2.0m North-South and 2.5m East-West. This natural energy grid has nodal points separated by 2.0m in North-South direction and by 2.5m in East-West direction, resulting in formation of distinct areas of positive energy and negative energy depending on the base level of the grid. Due to raised thermal activity, this B.E.M. grid gets distorted, leading to shift in natural position of nodal points.

If excavations are carried out and pits or basements located in South zone, the B.E.M. grid gets distorted resulting in severe dislocations due to thermal variation during daytime. *Vastushastra* considers pits or excavations in the South and Southwest zone as 'sins of planning' and advises raised plinth levels and loading in these zones.

The disturbed geomagnetic flux lines entangled in distorted B.E.M. grid result in chaotic energy contours hazardous to organic life - a process known in mythological terms as *'Shiv-Tandav'*.

Forces, Fields, and Vastu

The symbolic deities governing various directions in *Vastu-Purush-Mandal* represent the results of interacting 'Jaivik' and 'Pranik' forces. The ordered, disciplined electromagnetic field as existing in the North and East zones represent 'Godhead' or 'bliss of nature'. The disordered electromagnetic field patterns observed in the South, Southwest zones represent the 'curse of nature'.

2.3 Source and Sink Directions, and Vastu

2.3.1 Directions and Sub-Directions

The East, West, North, and South are called as the main directions of a Vastu, while Northeast, Southeast, Northwest, and Southwest are the sub-directions. The main directions of a Vastu represent streams of specific energies. Since these directions act as source or sink for energies, orientation and alignment of forces are predetermined in their zones of influence. In absence of such constraints, sub-directions of a Vastu play an important role in *Vastushastra*. Sub-directions represent zones of confluence of two different energy streams, which are at right angles to each other. As such, any disturbance in flow in any sub-direction initiates turbulence in energy flow, which is aligned to the main directions. In ancient texts, sub-directions are called *Marma-Sthan*, loosely translated as *Focal Points*.

The East and the North represent source directions for *'Pranik'* and *'Jaivik'* energy flows respectively, While the West and the South are sinks for these energies. This leads to the following source-sink combinations;

Northeast -> Source + Source
Southeast -> Source + Sink
Southwest -> Sink + Sink
Northwest -> Sink + Source

```
                    Pranik Urja
                ↓ ↓ ↓ ↓ ↓ ↓
              NE      E      SE
     J  →   ┌─────────────────┐
     a  →   │                 │
     i      │                 │
     v  →   │                 │
     i      │  ┌───┐          │
     k  →   │N │   │        S │
     U  →   │  │   │          │
     r      │  │VASTU│        │
     j  →   │  └───┘          │
     a      │                 │
            └─────────────────┘
              NW     W      SW
```

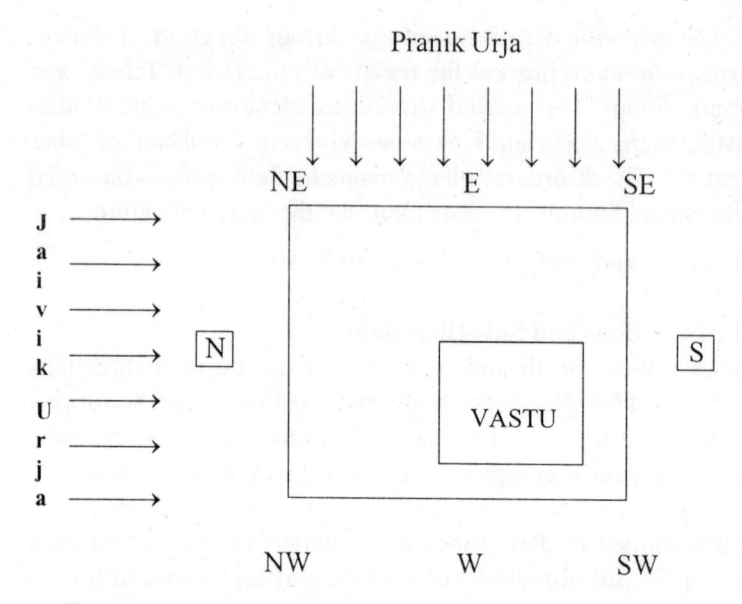

Fig.2.2: Energy source and sink directions for a Vastu

Since Northeast is a source-source focal point, minimum or no load in this zone and maximum side margins leads to ample positive energy flow for the Vastu.

Southwest is a sink-sink focal point. As such, maximum possible loading in this zone along with minimum possible side margins allows for balancing the energy-matter equation.

Similarly, comparatively reduced charges are indicated for the Southeast and Northwest zones, which are sink-source and source-sink focal points respectively.

Since sub-directions act as focal points ('*Marma-Sthan*') of energy source-sink, positioning of windows, ventilators, and loads in these zones needs careful attention while planning a *Vastu*. In general, we can visualise source of energy as a sink of matter, and source of matter as a sink of energy. Planning as per Vastu-science becomes easy, once this source-sink logic is seen and understood in terms of energy-matter balance.

2.3.2 Aura of Directions

Main directions North and south are related to geomagnetic organic flow. East and West are related to solar Pranik flow. Hence flow in main direction has direct effect on one stream only. Traditionally sub-directions are termed *Marma Sthan* i.e. the most effective zones, as any flow in sub-directions contributes to disturbance in both streams. A fault in sub-direction leads to cut and break in the flow of cosmic helix of energy.

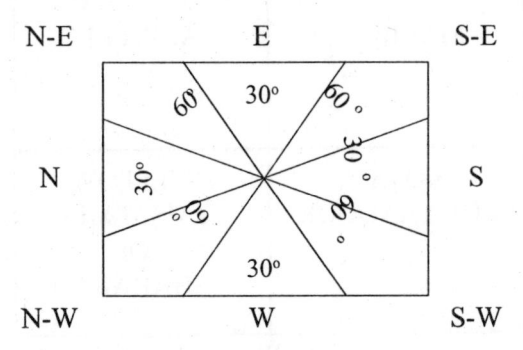

Fig.2.3: Zones of Influence for Directions

Extrapolating the above logic, a single point is allotted to main direction and two points to sub-directions. In a spherical sky of 360°, there are in all twelve points allotted for main and sub-directions combined, one point representing 30° of surrounding space. This implies that main direction control 30° of immediate space, while the sub-directions rule over 60° of adjacent space.

This clearly proves that the area of the main direction is limited to 30° and the area of sub-direction is focused on 60°. This fact is evident in natural horoscope where two houses are allotted to sub-direction and one house is allotted to main direction.

This is the reason that in *Dwar-Nivesh-Phal* main doors are not situated in the zones of sub-directions. '*Dwar-Nivesh-Phal*' which helps in determining the position of the main entrance to the Vastu, takes complete care of the hidden source-sink and energy-matter relationship. The specific deities, virtues, and vices in Dwar Nivesh Phal (fig. 16.7) symbolically represent the micro variations in the energy levels.

2.3.3 Directions and Flooring Pattern

Selection of flooring materials and patterns can be finalised by making use of the qualities of the five great elements, energy source-sink relationship, and energy-matter equation as applied to the sub-directions.

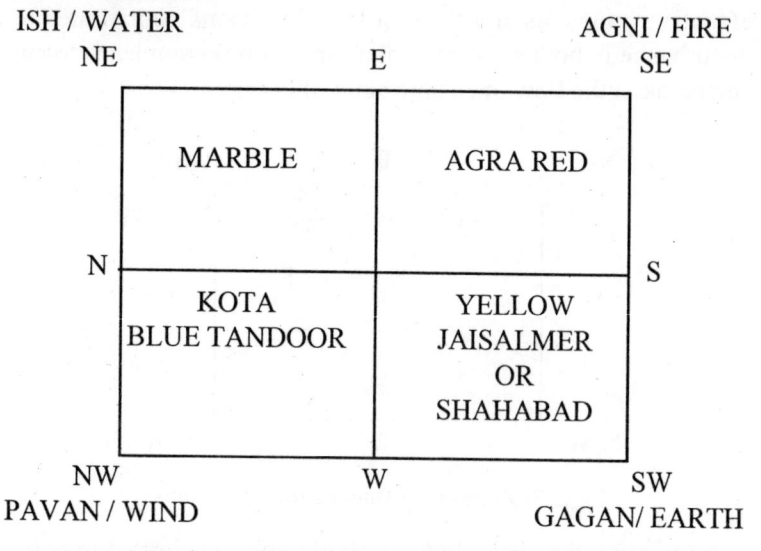

```
ISH / WATER                               AGNI / FIRE
   NE                  E                      SE
      +-----------------+------------------+
      |                 |                  |
      |     MARBLE      |    AGRA RED      |
      |                 |                  |
   N  +-----------------+------------------+  S
      |      KOTA       |     YELLOW       |
      |  BLUE TANDOOR   |   JAISALMER      |
      |                 |       OR         |
      |                 |    SHAHABAD      |
      +-----------------+------------------+
   NW                   W                     SW
PAVAN / WIND                             GAGAN / EARTH
```

Fig.2.4: Flooring Pattern Based on VPM and Qualities of Five Great Elements

The role of primary directions and sub-directions in determining *Pranik Urja* and *Jaivik Urja* flow characteristics has already been discussed in this chapter. The flooring pattern is selected in such a manner that these two streams create positive energy envelope for the Vastu.

White marble reflects and polarises electromagnetic energy, specifically sunlight. Therefore, to enhance the positive energy sources, white marble is the best material for flooring in the Northeast zone. From other angle, white is a colour of '*Jal-Tatwa*' as per *Yogashastra*. Hence, use of white marble in the Northeast zone provides the qualities of '*Jal-Tatwa*' to this zone, as required.

stone, provides the necessary loading to compensate energy sink and the red colour representing '*Agni-Tatwa*' satisfies the requirements of this zone. If Agra Red is not available, any pink coloured flooring can act as substitute.

For the Southwest zone, yellow coloured flooring - Yellow Jaisalmer or Yellow Shahabad stone - are recommended. Yellow represents '*Prithvi-Tatwa*', the Earth element. This type of flooring orients the 'Gurutwa' (heaviness) towards this zone for the necessary compensation through matter source to offset the sink-sink combination for energy in the Southwest zone. As per the Chinese Feng-Shui, yellow carpets in this zone give very good results. Raised plinth levels in the Southwest zone can also provide the necessary heavy loading for this zone.

Kota or blue Tandoor stone is generally used for flooring in the Northwest zone. It is to be noted that blue or green colour represents the 'wind' element, matching the qualitative requirements of the Northwest zone.

Here, we discussed the relevance of main directions and sub-directions in terms of *Pranik Urja* and *Jaivik Urja*. Once the flaws or deficiencies are assessed for different directions, it is an easier task to use the qualities of *Panch-Maha-Bhutas* for suitable remedial measures for the Vastu.

3. COSMIC ENERGY AND VASTU

3.1 Energy Dynamics

Vastushastra essentially deals with two energy sources - the solar energy flux and the geomagnetic energy flux. The science of Vastu aims at controlling the flow of these energies in a Vastu by selecting proper directions and alignments for the Vastu. Location of windows, walls, doors, loads, colour schemes, flooring and zoning, planting of trees - all these parameters play their part in enhancing the energy field for the human being to live in harmony with nature.

All bio-chemical actions, as also mental thought processes can be traced to some basic molecular activity at cellular level. Vastu-science, through manipulation of natural forces, brings some order to these life-processes. For human existence, any change at cosmic level is reflected in changes in cellular rhythm and vice versa.

Eastern concepts of building construction are closely related to Nature and natural energies. Vastu-science is directed towards forming of cosmic envelope, which is devoid of any negative energy fields, so that a Vastu is bestowed with peace and bliss. Enhancement of positive energies and subtraction of negative energies in Vastushastra provide environmental enrichment.

The Eastern thought is based on the concept of *holistic harmony* wherein every attempt is made to improve the positive effects of the four parameters - vibrations, waves, sound, and light.

Vibration: Any motion that repeats itself in equal intervals of time is called periodic motion. Periodic motion is often termed as harmonic motion. If a particle in a periodic motion moves back and forth over the same path, the motion is called *oscillatory* or *vibratory*. In most of the mechanical systems, an oscillating body cannot maintain its movement between fixed points because of dissipation of energy of motion on account of frictional forces.

This type of damping can be removed by feeding energy into the oscillating system so as to compensate the energy loss due to friction.

Balance wheel of a watch, sitar strings, atoms in a molecule or solid lattices are a few examples of commonly known oscillating systems. Radio waves, microwaves and visible light are oscillating magnetic and electrical field vectors.

Vibrations at cellular level in mind and body play an important role in considerations that go into defining principles of *Yogashastra* and *Vastushastra*.

Waves: The vibratory motion in a continuum in relation to time and space is represented by waves. The ocean waves, undulating outward moving ripples in a lake or a river are the phenomenon that can be observed with naked eye. The electromagnetic and the pressure waves are not directly visible, but can be experienced through the phenomena like light and sound.

The waves can be said to represent positive energy or negative energy depending on life-enhancing or life-destroying characteristics of the waves. The harmonic polarised waves have always proved beneficial to the life processes, while the random chaotic waves create obstructions in a smoothly flowing life pattern.

Sound: The human ear perceives any sound as melody or noise on the basis of constructive or destructive interaction of waves. The interference of waves results in various interesting phenomena - the modulation of wave packet with relation to amplitude and frequency, the resonating wave patterns etc. The ancient Hindu sciences studied the micro effects of sound on human body and mind and have emphasised the importance of primordial sounds like '*Aum*', the '*Mantras*' and the '*Beejaksharas*' in bringing about positive changes in the human dimension in particular and critical changes in any life process, in general. The well-known concepts of '*Halos*' or '*Aura*' around a person can be traced to the sound energy working at micro-cellular level.

Light: Modern science knows 'light' as a component of electromagnetic spectrum. The phenomenon of light is generally associated with electromagnetic radiation that affects the eye. In the spiritual dimension 'the light' is some holistic knowledge that has to be attained. It is said that, the person who chants the key Vedic '*Mantras*' rhythmically, can visualise the particular scene or picture, the particular colour or '*Jyoti*' that is associated with the '*Mantra*'. As pointed out earlier, the mind is termed as '*Tejas Dravyam*' in '*Upanishads*' and human consciousness is holistically correlated with light and energy.

The edicts of '*Vastushastra*' strive to annihilate the negative energy fields and to enhance the positive, creative energy forms suitable for human mind and body. Harmony with natural vibrations, rhythmic patterns through sound waves, and polarised energy fields through light are the basic aspects of '*Vastushastra*' principles.

The ancient practice of symbolising scientific concepts in terms of Goddesses, deities, shapes, forms or rituals has shrouded this source of knowledge in an aura of mystery. The logic behind these symbols has been lost over a period of time through the rapid changes in the life-style and social patterns in the human society subjected to natural or man-made calamities.

We will now try to unfold the mystery surrounding these symbols in the light of ancient knowledge and modern scientific logic. Specific subjects that will be discussed are - cosmic energy, energy imbalance, matter imbalance, concept of helix etc.

3.2 Inverted Volcano of Cosmic Energy

In geological terms, a volcano is a mountain or a hill having openings in earth's crust through which lava, cinders, steam, gases are expelled intermittently or continuously. But, in life and literature, the term 'volcano' is associated with suppressed feelings or state of affairs which are likely to cause violent outburst.

An interesting aspect of volcanic activities is, greater the load matter atop the lava, lesser the chances of volcanic eruptions.

Cosmic, Energy and Vastu 17

This concept was used by the old master-designers of *Vastushastra* to create a type of inverted volcano on houses through deft manipulation of directions. The South, the Southwest and the West are directions involved in inverted volcano. Even the modern scientific research points out that these directions are subjected to excessive cosmic particle activity. Conventionally, the North is 'source' and the South is 'sink' for electromagnetic flux lines. Sub-atomic particles travelling along the geomagnetic flux lines end-up at the southern tip. The East-West asymmetry effect in nuclear physics acknowledges the fact that excessive cosmic radiation particles, particularly, positively charged particles, enter the earth's atmosphere from the West rather than the East.

In the Indian sub-continent, every house is subjected to excessive solar radiation from the Southeast, South, and Southwest directions, while the North, Northeast, and East sides are in the shadow region. This high thermal imbalance can disturb the smooth pattern of geomagnetic flux lines to create a mesh of crossing flux lines with attendant nodal points which can trap sub-atomic particles to emit radiation harmful to life-processes.

Vastushastra suggests remedies to offset the chaotic conditions in the Southern zone. The specific measures include;
- avoiding openings towards the South direction,
- provision of thick or cavity walls on the South side,
- planting of trees in the South, especially, 'Audumber' type trees that exhale water vapours,
- reduction in the South side margins,
- providing greater height and thickness to the South and the Southwest compound walls,
- constructing extra floor on the South side, with terraces towards the North and the East,
- proscribing any bore-wells, basements, and under-ground water tanks on the South side,
- elevating the plinth levels of the South side rooms,
- placing heavy furniture, cabinets, and loads in the South and Southwest zones,

- elevating the South and the Southwest zones through rocks, stones and heavy loads in landscaping.

3.3 Vortex of Energy Imbalance

A vortex is a mass of rotating or whirling fluid. Whirlpool in water and whirlwind in air are the common examples. In physics, vortex is synonymous with a portion of fluid whose particles have rotating motion. Enormous destructive linear forces are unleashed on any object in the vicinity of the centrifugal axis of the vortex. Vortices in oceans can swallow large ships. Vortex in a tornado or a typhoon can uproot trees, destroy houses. In other words, a vortex is a source of tremendous negative energy. Here, we will study the concept of cosmic vortex and how its linear forces attack a Vastu.

In *Vastushastra*, it is possible to find a remedy if the imbalance in forces triggering the formation of vortex is suitably analysed. The thermal imbalance around a house is one such source of vortex, which can easily be untwisted. By balancing the negative forces acting on a Vastu through solid matter as a static equaliser, it possible to avoid any kind of vortex.

Let us now try to find out the manner in which thermal imbalance disturbs and creates a twist in energy flow around a house.

As far as solar radiation is concerned, the Northwest, North, and Northeast zones are in shadow region and as such, are in complete thermal balance. Low level of thermal activity in these zones allows undisturbed flow of geomagnetic flux lines. The undisturbed, balanced and cool areas of the Northern zones achieves the rhythm and harmony beneficial to human mind and body.

In *Vastu-Purush-Mandal Pavan*, Soma, and Ish the virtuous Deities are assigned to these directions only. Yogashastra specifies these very directions as zones of Ida or Chandra Nadi, which represents all the positive life processes. In astrological considerations, the fourth house in a horoscope is associated with Northern directions and represents happiness in life.

As seen in Fig.3.1, temperatures start climbing as we shift from the East to Southeast, South, and Southwest. Solar radiation is highest

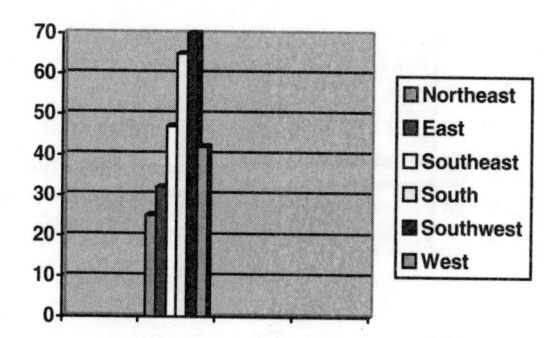

Fig. 3.1: Relative thermal activity for different zones

in the Southern zone, giving rise to excessive thermal activity, which triggers imbalance in natural forces. It is as if we are moving along a spiral staircase of increasing thermal activity from Northeast to East, East to Southeast, Southeast to South, and South to Southwest. In other words, we encounter rising imbalance of forces and distorted geomagnetic field around a house as we move from the stable Northeast zone to the extremely disturbed Southwest zone. In *Vastu-Purush-Mandal*, the Southern directions are ruled by the deities of destruction - *Agni, Yama*, and *Niruta*.

3.4 Cyclic Helix of Matter Balance

To contain these vortices of cosmic and thermal imbalances, Vastushastra offers a remedy in the form of the 'Helix' concept. Helix, the natural growth shape is known as the mystery and the magic of the almighty. The Helix as a mystic symbol finds references in all the ancient scriptures throughout the world. In the Aryan culture, the symbol '*Aum*' is a confluence of three spirals or helices. In Chinese culture Yin-Yang represents a double helix. 'Guru' or 'Master', the highest form of enlightenment is described as '*Akhand Mandalakaram*' i.e. a continuous spiral without a beginning or an end. Peter Stevens in his book 'Patterns of Nature' has rightly said; "The helix is the height of versatility playing roles in the replication of the smallest virus and in the arrangement of matter in the largest Galaxy."

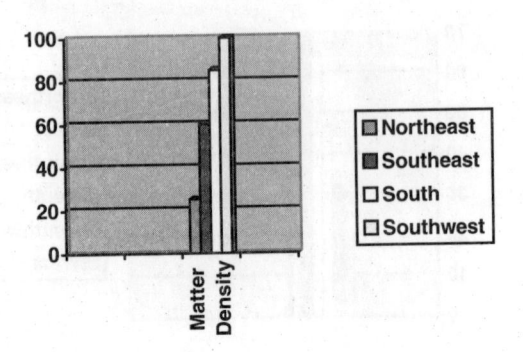

Fig.3.2: Relative matter density for different directions

As indicated in Fig. 3.2, *Vastushastra* specifies a specific set of matter density, loading, and openings for the specific directions aligned with a house. The least possible load should be in the Northeast direction. The loading should increase with spiralling staircase of energy imbalance towards the Southeast, South, and Southwest. Blockage of openings should also follow the same pattern.

Just by adhering to the following rules, it is possible to implement the Helix concept in a house;

* Align the entire house in the Southwest zone with maximum side margin to the North and the East. This ensures loading of South and Southwest zones of a plot.
* Provide underground water tank or boring-well in the North or Northeast zone to achieve reduction in matter and loading in the geomagnetically stable and balanced Northeast zone. Thus, the capacity of the Northeast zone to act as the source of all positive energies is substantially increased.
* More terrace areas should be located in the North, Northeast, and East zones. Roof slopes and ground slopes should be from the Southern and Western zones towards the Northern and Eastern zones.

* To maintain the original balanced state of energy fields, no trees should be planted in the North, Northeast, and East zones.
* With the starting point as the Northeast corner, more floors should be added towards the Southwest zone. In the building elevation, the Northeast should be the lowest point and the Southwest the highest.
* The basic plinth level should be increasing towards the Southeast, South, and Southwest and should gradually be reduced towards the West, Northwest, and the North.

3.5 Energy Forms - Multidisciplinary Approach

A characteristic correlation is evident in identification of energy forms in various disciplines like *Yogashastra*, Astrology, *Vastushastra*, and Modern Science. The topic has separately been discussed under chapters on *Yoga-Vastu* and *Astro-Vastu*. Here, we try to understand the significance of the underlying common features.

In Yogashastra, two streams of energy are associated with the Moon and the Sun though the *Ida* and the *Pingala nadis*. The north zone is under the control of '*Ida*' and the south under '*Pingala*'. The central stream called *Brahma* or *Shushubhna* nadi is generally dormant. This stream links the individual and the cosmos to form a single unified energy field or the *Akshayatwa*. All the good happenings and bliss is linked to the flow of '*Ida*' and all the cruelty and hardship is related to the '*Pingala*' stream.

In Astrology, the fourth house in horoscope, with the Moon as the owner, represents the North point and is called '*Sukhsthan*' - an abode of happiness. While, the tenth house representing the South point, is called '*Karmasthan*' - an abode of hardship. The Sun in its devastating radiation stage at noon lies in the tenth house. Saturn, the son of the Sun, rules the South point.

From the above discussions, it is evident that the references to the directions in Yogashastra match with those in Astrology.

In *Vastu-Purush-Mandal*, all deities are identified by names related to the positive or the negative confluence of the two energy sources - the Sun and the Moon. The North region is represented by deities having positive energies and good, divine, and auspicious effects. On the other hand, deities with negative energies represent the South region.

Positive confluence of two energy streams is similar to constructive interference in science, where summation of positive energies takes shape to enhance free flow characteristics of both the streams. The negative confluence results in destructive interference where loss of energy at anti-node points leads to impediment, obstruction, and friction to the flow of individual energies. When the Sun is in the North, the *'Jaivik Urja'* (organic energy) and *'Pranik Urja'* (solar energy) flow in the same direction spreading positive energies in the environment. In contrast, when the Sun is in the South, the organic and the solar energies are in mutually opposite directions, spewing negative energies in the surrounding space.

Finer the element or subtle the energy, wider is the effect of the great element. Amongst the five great elements, sky or ether is the most powerful and the elements fire, wind, water, and earth have reducing degree of effectiveness.

All remedies recommended in *Avak-Hada Chakra* are based on sky (ether) element. If used skilfully, these are direct and more powerful than other remedies. The mass-energy equivalence and wave-particle duality concepts in modern science imply that rhythmic movement of particles in an energy field can enhance the positive energies through resonance effect. Polarisation of energies, i.e., the unidirectional flow coherent in time and/or space, results in disciplined ordered flow necessary for consolidated action.

4. YOGASHASTRA CONCEPTS IN VASTU SCIENCE

4.1 Yogashastra and Vastushastra

Eastern thinking considers Vastu to be a living soul acting as a companion to the Vastu occupants. In the Hindu ethos, every Goddess is invariably associated with its own divine vehicle or chariot - Nandi the carrier of Shiva, Lotus the carrier of Laxmi and Brahma, Garuda the carrier of Vishnu etc. This divine relationship is also evident between a person and his home. The ritual of Vastushanti aims at removing negative elements from living space inside the Vastu and replacing these with constructive cosmic powers.

When we consider the flow of energy within a Vastu and the role of deities associated with Vastu directions, remarkable similarity between the concepts of *Yogashastra* and *Vastushastra* can be perceived.

Yogashastra speaks of three basic energy streams in a human body;
* *Ida*, the Chandra Nadi
* *Pingala*, the Surya Nadi
* *Shushubhna*, the Brahma Nadi

Ida stream is associated with the North and the East directions. This stream is considered as bliss flowing from material happiness and contentment of the five senses. New beginnings should be made, good work initiated, and important decisions taken only in the stream of Ida nadi.

As per *Vastushastra* guidelines, a house or a dwelling should be constructed on a plot in such a manner that extra side margins are available to the East and the North. This ensures that Pranik bliss is bestowed on all the occupants. In *Vastu-Purush-Mandal*, Soma (Moon) is the deity of the North direction. In Astrology, the fourth house in a horoscope represents peace and happiness. This house is governed by Moon and the associated zodiac sign Cancer represents the North direction. This concept is reflected in *Vastushastra*, which considers all houses with large side margins and openings to the North and the East directions as heavenly abodes.

Pingala or the *Surya nadi* has correlation with the South and West directions. This stream represents all the evil, cruel, and inhuman trends with bad omens at every stage of life. It is not advisable to think of new beginnings or important decisions when the *Surya nadi* is active. During the *Pingala* flow, a common thing like departure from a place can also prove to be harmful.

The three streams link the micro level human consciousness with the cosmic consciousness. From another point of view, the five basic elements (*Panch-Maha-Bhutas*) at macro level representing the cosmic power are in total conformity with human beings at micro level during the *Ida* flow. This is the period when Preeti-Sangam of different elements in nature takes place, leading to cosmic bliss. These streams serve as key to instinctive self-preservation techniques made available to the human beings by the nature itself. *Vastushastra* creates pathways to achieve unhindered natural flow of cosmic energies in a Vastu in harmony with these three streams.

The *Ida* stream associated with the North and East directions is considered beneficial in *Vastushastra*. As against this, the *Pingala* stream representing the South and West is avoided while planning a house. Least possible side margins to the West and South, with minimum or no openings to these directions and placing of heavy loading in the South, Southwest, and West zones helps in cutting-off *Pingala* stream and retaining only the positive energies inside the house.

Reverting to astrology, we find that the master of the tenth house in a horoscope is Saturn, representing negative powers. Saturn has ownership over the Southern horizon and powers over the Western horizon. Creating excess margins on the South and the West invites permanent shadow of Saturn over the household, leading to pain, sorrow and losses.

The flow of Ida and Pingala alternately changing over short intervals in a continuous stream is termed as Brahma Nadi or Shushubhna stream. In *Yogashastra*, Shushubhna has direct correlation with the entire cosmic reality, which is totally different from the observable worldly phenomena. *Yogashastra* advocates silence, meditation, and alertness of mind during the Shushubhna flow. This stream represents fresh beginnings and a perspective beyond the *Ida* and *Pingala* flows.

4.2 Vastu Nabhi

Vastu Nabhi is the cosmic naval connection between the microcosm, the Vastu and the macrocosm, the Nature. Definition of the correct location of the *Brahma Nabhi* depends on the orientation of the five great elements in the right locations in and around the Vastu. A deep study of the qualities of directions in relation to Astrology and *Yogashastra* is the key to correctly positioning the Brahma Nabhi in the Vastu. The form of natural helix as clubbed with the qualities of the directions and the five great elements can define the right location of the *Vastu Nabhi*. Deities and demons as indicated in the *Vastu-Purush-Mandal*, the two stream theory, the concept of source and sink directions, classification of the five great elements as related to the specific directions are the foundation stones of the concept of *Brahma Vastu Nabhi*.

Correct alignment of the *Vastu Nabhi* initiates the cosmic divine connection along the source directions. As per the Vastu rules, the clockwise helix of matter is counter balanced with the anticlockwise helix of energy. Matter helix has sink end in the Northeast zone, and the source end in the Southwest zone. Since the Northeast is a source direction in *Vastushastra*, shower of cosmic energy on the Northeast point multiplies the blessings due to the right handed helix of matter as defined by the *Vastushastra*.

The mysterious cosmic breath is closely linked with the helix, the Vastu Nabhi, and the Brahma. The element Akash (sky) which is event manifest, descends effortlessly along with the cosmic Pranik energy through the Northeast cosmic door of the Vastu and flows without friction, blockage, or impedance along the Vastu helix, for union with the cosmic breath and revitalisation of the *Brahma Vastu Nabhi*.

Vastushastra maintains that heavy loads, columns, or pillars should strictly be avoided in the zone of Brahma to keep this mystic flow in a dormant state. It is further pronounced that a ceiling or a roof, to cut off the contact between the micro level Brahma stream and the macro level Shushubhna stream flowing in the cosmos, should cover the Brahmasthan.

4.3 Ida, Pingala, and Directions

We will now elaborate on the concept of the three nadis. *Ida* has control over East and North directions. All good things, all creative works, arts and research, religious and life promoting activities are attributed to the flow of *Ida Nadi* (left or northern current flow). *Pingala* i.e. Surya Nadi has control over West and South directions. All violent activities, all destructive forces, deployment of weapons, tortures, sorrows, cruel and tough jobs, worldly attractions are attributed to the flow of *Surya* or *Pingala Nadi* (right or south flow). Brahma or Madhyam Nadi represents only the holy and devotional duties, i.e., reading religious scriptures, meditation, prayers and absence of worldly material activities. In other words, maintaining *Ida* flow is good, divine and worldly bliss. To block Pingala flow is to avoid destruction and disturbances. Vastushastra recommends that maximum space should be left open towards the North and the East directions and that the Vastu should be aligned in the South and West zones. Provision of more space in the North and the East directions ensures that the entire household is exposed to health preserving energy of clear morning sun for the maximum possible duration. Maximum openings to East and North maintain and shower this bliss on the entire house. Absence of openings to the South and the Southwest as stated in *Vastushastra* cross ventilates this positive energy from the East to the North, and like a circular flow, from the North to the East. For a house with minimum side margins to the South and the West on the rearside effectively blocks any *Pingala Nadi* current and adds all good effects of *Ida* Nadi by maintaining flow in North and East directions only.

To achieve the dynamic stability by equalising gravitational forces, magnetic flux effect and to attain environmental purity and a sense of cosmic reality, major load of the house should be aligned to the South and the West zones of the plot.

As seen in previous chapters, a loaded South can absorb the cosmic elementary particles travelling along the magnetic field lines and can reduce the deleterious micro radiations. Thick walls without openings on the South side provide a shield to the household against this destructive cosmic force.

Yogashastra asserts that just by maintaining a perfect posture of body, substantial qualities are added to body, mind, and intellect. Similarly, simple alignment and positioning of a house in proper zone of a plot as per *Vastushastra* can add several qualities to the house or a dwelling.

4.4 Insight into Yoga-Vastu

The flow of *Prana* through a human body and the flow of cosmic energy through a *Vastu* are in essence parallel concepts.

According to *Yogashastra*, the universe is composed of two substances: *Akash* (ether) and *Prana* (cosmic energy). Everything that has a form, or is the result of a combination evolves out of Akash. It is the '*Akash* that becomes the air, liquids, solids, the human body, animals, plants etc. Everything we can touch, all the forms we see, everything that exists can be sourced to the *Akash*. It is so subtle that we cannot perceive it, for it is visible only after it has taken form. The power by which it is transformed into the universe is *Prana*.

Everything we call energy or force evolves out of *Prana*. In all forms of life, from the highest to the lowest, the *Prana* is present as a living force. Every force is based on *Prana*, it is the origin of movement, gravity, magnetism, physical action, the nerve currents and the force of thought. *Prana* is the soul of all force and energy and there can be no life without it. It is found in the air, water and food. *Prana* is the vital force inside each living being, and 'thought' is considered to be the highest and the most refined action of *Prana*. *Prana* is said to concentrate at the point where our mind is focused.

"प्राणो ब्रह्मेति व्यजानात्" (*Prano Brahmeti Vyajanat*). In *Taitiraya Upanishad* it is said that the whole existence is based on *Prana*, is part of 'Prana' and it ends in '*Prana*'. '*Prana*' belongs to one of the five elements of *Panch-Maha-Bhutas* i.e. Vayu. It exists in the human body in five more types - *Prana, Apana, Vyan, Udan,* and *Saman*. These five are correlated with five basic elements - *Akash, Vayu, Tej, Udak* and *Prithvi*.

Prarabdha defines the relationship, the unbroken link an individual has established with the eternal nature. The breathing process of a man is essentially preordained by the impetus provided by *Prarabdha* and the breathing itself determines the overall emotional make-up of the person. Even the relative effects of the planets, constellations and zodiac on the individual are subject to the vigour of his breath as determined by the flow of *Prana*. The course taken by *Prarabdha* flow qualifies the nature of *Vastu-sukh* (bliss ensuing from a dwelling) an individual is entitled to. A horoscope, which is a reflection of *Prarabdha* in time, can therefore successfully be used for describing or predicting the type of dwelling a person may possess.

Existence of cosmic energy in a human body is the amalgamation of these five elements with the five *Prana*. The Home, the Vastu which serves as a shield of human body, is taken care of by Vastushastra on the same basic logic that applies to *Panch-Prana* and the five basic elements. Basic rules and regulations in *Shiv Swarodaya Shastra* to preserve and enlighten the 'Godliness' in human body are applicable to *Vastushastra* also. The science of *Yoga* maintains a correlation between existence, reality and truth by effective flow of *Panch-Prana*. The rules of *Vastushastra* beneficially applied, attempt to maintain balance with cosmic reality, to illuminate intelligence and to attain peace by following perfect directions, perfect magnetic flux and perfect coordination of the basic five elements.

In **Yogashastra**, the flow of *Prana* in the body is correlated with virtues of five basic elements and qualities of five elements in relation to human body are also defined. Colour, shape, taste and smell of five elements are categorised in Yogashastra. Amongst

Yogashastra Concepts in Vastu Science

these colours, shapes, tastes and smells; *Vastushastra* defines qualities associated with *Prithvi* and *Jal tatva* as good and those with *Agni-Tej* as unhealthy, while qualities with *Vayu tatva* are considered as inert. This classification matches the scientifically analysed mineral-content in the soil acceptable for use in the base of the *Vastu*.

Any abode demands contribution of all the qualitative parameters like colour, taste, shape, form, sound and touch. All these qualities are attributed to *Prithvi-Tatva* alone. Hence, *Vastu* science gives importance to influencing expression of *Prithvi-Tatva*. Here, we see how foundations of Vastu concepts have been derived from *Yogashastra*. A deep understanding and right selection makes it possible to match definitions in *Yogashastra* and applications in *Vastushastra*.

Element (Tatva)	Colour (Varna)	Shape (Akar)	Taste (Swad)	Quality (Guna)
Earth (Prithvi)	Yellow	Square/Rectangle	Sweet (Madhur)	Good
Water (Jal)	White	Semi-circle	Salty (Turat)	Good
Fire (Agni)	Red	Triangle	Hot (Tikshna)	Inert
Air (Vayu)	Blue/Black	Circle	Acidic (Amla)	Bad
Ether (Akash)	Not defined	None	Bitter (Kadu)	Bad

Table 4.1: Characteristics and Qualities of Panch-Maha-Bhuta (Five Great Elements)

Drawing from the *Yogashastra* insight, *Vastushastra* allots specific characteristics to the five basic elements. The element 'Earth' is visualised as yellow-coloured, 'Water' as white, 'Fire' as red, 'Wind' as blue, and the 'Ether' as having no definite colour with property to borrow colour from any other element.

The classification and characteristics of these elements can be described (Table 4.1) in terms of *varna* (colour), *akar* (shape), *swad* (taste) and *guna* (quality).

Panch-Maha-Bhutas (Five Great Elements)	Prithvi (Earth), Aap (Water), Tej (Fire), Vayu (Air), Akash (Ether)
Tanmatras (Five Subtle Elements)	Roop (Form), Rasa (Taste), Gandha (Smell), Sparsh (Touch), Shabda (Sound)
Gunas (Qualities & Evolutionary Powers)	Sattva (Illumination), Rajas (Activity), Tamas (Dormancy) **Form:** Mahat (Cosmic Intellect)
	Ahamkara (Ego), Buddhi (Intellect), Manas (Mind) **Form:** Chitta (Consciousness)
Jnanendriyas (Five Organs of Perception)	Ears, Eyes, Nose, Tongue, Skin
Karmendriyas (Five Senses of Action)	Legs, Arms, Speech, Excretory Organs, Reproductive Organs

Table 4.2: Elements of Vedic Origin Reflected in Vastushastra Concepts

Basic Element	Vedic Scripture	Nature of Hymns
Earth (Prithvi)	Rigveda	Vibrations (Spandan)
Water (Jal)	Yajurveda	Waves (Valaya)
Fire (Agni)	Atharvaveda	Light (Prakash)
Air (Vayu)	Samveda	Sound (Dhwani)

Table 4.3: Correlation between Great Elements and Energy Forms in Vedic Scriptures

Yogashastra Concepts in Vastu Science

Yogashastra	Astrology	Vastushastra	Modern Science
Shanmukhi mudra gives knowledge about qualities of the five great basic elements.	Cosmos is divided into basic eight directions with twelve sectors of zodiac signs.	Vibrations, waves sound, and light are the active parameters in this science.	Explains qualities of * polarised energy forms, * laws of energy conservation, * mind-matter relationship,
The three main energy streams categorise the virtuous qualities of the eight directions.	These signs are classified on the basis of five basic elements. The directions are correlated with qualities of the five great elements interpreted in terms of beneficial colours, plants, gems and metallic base elements.	Qualities are classified, based on orientation, directions and energy sources. Qualities of directions can be improved on the basis of the five great elements.	Classification based on four types of forces - electro-weak, strong nuclear, electromagnetic, and gravitation. Processes are explained in terms of thermodynamics, entropy, particle-wave duality, energy transitions, energy-matter transformations etc.
Ida (Chandra Nadi) - Northeast **Pingala** (Surya Nadi) - Southwest **Sushubhna** (Brahma nadi) - Central Zone			Modern science can unveil the secrets of ancient science, and give new remedial measures to rectify & remove Vastudoshas and to provide environmental enrichment.

Table 4.4: Vastushastra Equation with Yogashastra, Astrology, and Science

As discussed previously, the *Yogashastra* concepts of *Prana, Nabhi, Nadi, Chakra, Panch-Maha-Bhutas,* and *Panch-koshas* have definite correlation with principles of *Vastushastra*. In Yogashastra, the *Shanmukhi* Mudra provides the body with qualities of *Panch-Maha-Bhutas* (five basic elements) and three important streams or current *Ida, Pingala* and *Shushubhna* are associated with qualities of directions.

Vastushastra essentials are based on contributions from the *Panch-Maha-Bhutas* and directions, concepts basically associated with *Yogashastra*. Again in Astrology, direction is an important aspect with the directionally located *Rashis* (zodiac) and *Nakshatras* (constellations) having qualities of *Panch-Maha-Bhutas*. Further, the recommended *Aradhyavrikshas* (beneficial plants) for a given constellation have associated with them, definite colours, rhythms and qualities of the five basic elements. The chart (Table 4.4) indicates the comparative features of *Yogashastra*, Astrology and *Vastushastra*, and Modern Science. These characteristics peculiar to each of these disciplines, in a wider context of cosmic existence, provide correlating factors that make *Vastushastra* an all-encompassing science.

4.5 Yogashastra - Path to Contentment

The purpose of life is joy. Attaining this goal through finer and subtle means is possible through Yogashastra. Alleviating sorrow and unhappiness has been the divine duty of the five sub-branches of the *Darshanshastra*.

To search for remedy without understanding the causative factor is futile and insane. Causality, a subject studied in science, should be correlated with true knowledge to behold the light of universal truth. Perception is the reflection of *Pradnya* which is the polarised force of unified body, mind, and intellect. This 'oneness' is the subject matter of all the five sub-branches of *Darshanshastra*.

In *Upanishads*, mind is identified with '*Tejas Dravyam*', in Zen culture thought is assumed to be matter, and in modern science, the thought is considered an extension of mind. By its very nature, thought is always translated into some form of electromagnetic waves. As such, the mind has direct correlation with some specific energy field. A disturbed mind is represented by a chaotic pattern of electromagnetic signals devoid of any pattern, order, or rhythm.

Matter can behave as a particle or a wave. Because of equivalence of mass and energy, we can further say that energy manifests itself either as particles or as waves. If we consider the Zen concept 'Thought is matter', it is possible to transplant this mind-thought in a holistic divine envelope by external environmental enrichment brought about by applying basic life instincts in all human endeavours seeking to conquer the nature. This pattern is evident in all sub-branches of *Darshanshastra*.

In the present scenario, we find it very difficult to change the orientation of windows and doors in an existing flat or a place of residence. By treating the observed *Vastu-doshas* as a reflection of flaws pointed out by *Yogashastra*, it is possible to reduce the ill effects of incorrect streams in the house. Rather, *Yogic* remedies help in orienting the internal mind-body mechanism to fight the ill effects of *Vastu-doshas*.

We already have seen the correlation between the yogic stream Ida (Chandra Nadi) and the North direction. In case removing the obstacles blocking the North direction of a *Vastu* is not feasible, then doing the *Ida-Pranayam* as a reactive exercise can contribute towards regaining the lost rhythm in a *Vastu* due to Northern blockage. Externally also we can establish relationship between the human being and the cosmic North-stream. In Astrology, it is a common practice to use gemstone of opposite affiliated planet to compensate the lost vibrations due to a planet having negative influence on the horoscope. Same logic can be extended to align the two main streams in the body and the *Vastu*.

Pingala or the Surya Nadi is represented by the South direction. As per the Vastu-Purush-Mandal, openings towards the South direction facilitate *Yama-Pravah* in the *Vastu*, which places the *Jeeva* and *Prana* in mutual opposition. To compensate the loss of efficiency and biorhythm in a human being due to *Yama-Pravah*, regular *Pingala-Pranayam* exercise is advised. This *Pranayam* produces the right elements in the mind and body to fight the *Vastu-dosha* due to *Yama-Pravah*. *Pingala* stream is initiated in the human body when the body is in pain, hardship, and difficult rhythm. Activating the *Pingala* stream by *Pranayam* creates elements that can identify the pain and hardship to put up a determined fight against *Yama-Pravah*.

Yogis often use a supporting stick or '*Kubdi*' while sitting in a yogic posture. The *Kubdi* helps in activating the *Ida* or the *Pingala* stream through the pressure applied on the *nadis* in the armpit. Thus, Yogis can remain in any preferred stream for a long duration.

Yogashastra is based on the three basic elements - sound, wind, and space - that are identified as *Prana, Pavan,* and *Gagan*. *Yogashastra* provides mastery over Gagan (sky) - the most powerful and subtle element amongst the five basic elements. A regular Yogic practice of *Pranayam*, chanting of primordial sound such as '*Aum*', ringing of bells and sounding a conch (*Shankha*) are some of the remedial measures to offset the *Vastu-dosha*. A sensible *Vastushastra* approach always includes recourse to *Yogashastra* principles.

5. VASTU-DOSHA AND YOGIC REMEDIES

Vastu-dosha is a projected flaw or deficiency in the known characteristics of the eight directions. These directions have been endowed with qualities based on a classification sourced from the *Panch-Maha-Bhutas*. *Vastu-dosha* implies souring of qualities of the directions under consideration. In turn, *Vastu-dosha* is closely associated with the *Panch-Maha-Bhutas* related qualities of human body, mind, and soul. Through '*Sadhana*' or meditation, one can incorporate *Panch-Maha-Bhutas* related qualities of the directions in the human persona. On a microscopic level, these qualities can provide a shield emanating from the soul that can protect the person from ill effects of *Vastu-doshas*. This idea is particularly effective when human efforts found to be wanting on account of obstructions created by *Vastu-doshas* need additional propellant.

Indian *Darshanshastra* and spiritual disciplines describe many a mediation practices or '*Sadhana*' that can serve this very purpose. In this modern era, innovative meditation techniques, which are essentially offshoots of ancient practices, are gaining popularity. Although all these meditation techniques see 'salvation' as the final goal, the virtues experienced by human mind and body vary according to the characteristics of the specific methods. These subtleties in qualities and characteristics can be utilised as a form of Yogic remedy on *Vastu-dosha*.

The *Panch-Maha-Bhutas* concepts associate *Vastu-dosha* with the four basic elements - Earth (*Prithvi*), Water (*Jal*), Fire (*Tej*), and Wind (*Vayu*). Since the fifth element, Ether (*Akash*), is the most subtle and fundamental '*Maha-Bhuta*', it is said that 'one who wins control over '*Akash-tatva*' is not affected by the ill-effects of '*dosha*' (deficiency) in the *Prithvi*, *Jal*, *Tej*, and *Vayu* elements. The spiritual paths of enlightenment in a way focus on conquering the '*Akash-tatva*'. As such, a personal shield against effects of *Vastu-dosha* can be attained through spiritual regimens. The '*Siddha Purushas*' or the 'Enlightened' are not touched by any kind of *Vastu-dosha*. They conquer the mind and the 'self' and in the process cross the barriers of '*Mana*' (mind), '*Pavan*' (wind), and '*Gagan*' (ether) to establish control over the dominions of Nature and God.

Once the mind is brought under control through '*Sadhana*' (meditation), it frees itself from the shackles of space-time or in effect, from the influences of *Vastu-dosha*. The present day ownership-flat culture cannot guarantee layouts designed as per Vastu principles or provide amiable *Vastu* domain. Despite a difficult *Vastu* situation, a happy and contented life can be made possible through the Yogic and spiritual practices.

All types of Sadhana are powerful enough to transport the *Mana* (mind) to *Gagan* (ether). But, by correlating the self-evident virtues and direction related *dosha* (deficiency), certain *Sadhanas* have been prescribed to match with specific directional aspects.

Deficient Direction	Vidhi (Ritual) or Remedial Action
East	Arghyadan
Southeast	Yagna-yag
South	Sudarshan Kriya
Southwest & West	Reiki, Sun Worship, Yoga-Diksha, Shaktipat
Northwest	Pranayama
North	Vipasana
Northeast	Soham Sadhana

Table 5.1: Preferred Rituals for Specific Directions

Let us first consider the **East** direction.

5.1 Arghyadan (अर्घ्यदान)

A *Vastu* not receiving benefit of *Aditya Pravah* due to polluted East direction develops *Vastu-dosha*. *Aditya Pravah* is closely related with *Brahma Muhurta*. The concept of deficiency in the East direction implies deprivation of life-sustaining energies at the sunrise. As such, the traditional invocation of the Sun and *Arghyadan* is the best antidote on this type of Vastu-dosha.

The ritual of *Arghyadan* performed with water is associated with *Mantra, Namaskara, Vajrasana,* and *Pranayama*. The practice commences with cupping of water in hands and offering it to the Goddess Sun in a ritualistic manner at the predawn hours. The fingers, the palms, the arms are bestowed with the power of the Sun if one performs *Arghyadan* daily.

कराग्रे वसति लक्ष्मी:
करमध्ये सरस्वति
करमूलेतु गोविंदम्

Chinese acupressure technique also aims at recharging *Pranik* energy flow in the body through some nodal points on the palm. The focal point of spiralling energies in human body is located on the human palm itself. These centres receive cosmic energies in the process of *Arghyadan*. The recitation of *Beej Mantras* in *Suryopasana* (worshipping the Sun), the flow of *Aditya Shakti* in *Arghyadan*, and the *Nadi Shodhan* (purification of energy channels in body) in *Pranayama* initiates diffusion of *Pran Shakti* throughout the mind, intellect, and body to protect the person from any ill-effects of *Vastu-dosha*. Traditionally, *Arghyadan* is performed at early morning and evening twilight hours.

Not withstanding the fast paced current lifestyle, it is still possible to perform *Arghyadan* for 15 - 20 minutes daily on the terrace of a house to avail of remission from the flaws attributed to the polluted East direction.

5.2 Homa-Havan (होम हवन) - The Fire Worship

The imperfections in the Southeast direction are related to the anomalous combination of pollutants with the *Agni Tatva* (fire element). Traditionally proven *Vaishvadev Yag Havan* rituals aid in subsiding these flaws. The two types of *Havan Vidhi* (rituals) - customary (*Nitya*) and occasional (*Naimittik*) - performed with prescribed *Mantras*, burning of specific plants and shrubs in the divine fire, *Pranayama*, *Viniyog Nyas* and *Dhyan* create channels for circulation of *Pran Shakti* in the mind, body, intellect, and the *Vastu*. Realising the importance of these processes, our tradition has incorporated many such routines like *Udak Shanti*, *Graha Shanti* etc. spread over one's lifetime.

In modern times, positive changes brought about in the immediate environment through Havan have become a subject for scientific exploration. In Vedic culture, *Havan* is of utmost importance in all the rituals, religious ceremonies, and festivals. Symbolically, *Agni* or the fire is considered as mouth of the Divinity. In *Havan*, medicinal shrubs and plants are consigned to the flames through *Ahuti* and *Samidha*. The *Yagna* concepts refer to *Ashtadisha* (eight directions), *Ashtadikpal* (custodians of the eight directions) and other entities representing some thirty-three energy forms. The layout of the *Yagnakunda* (sacrificial altar) is in itself a distinct form of *Vastushastra* and its symbolic energy correlation is rather mysterious. The rituals include occult *Chakras*, colours, plants, shape of the altar, symbolic Goddess-energy correlation, circulation of *Prana* through *Panch-koshas* in *Nyas-Vidhi*, *Muhurta*, *Yama-Niyama* specified rhythmic recitation of Mantras, Arghyadan and finally the cosmic outlook in "अग्नये स्वाहा ॥ इदं न मम ॥". All these processes working at divine, earthly, and spiritual levels purify the mind, the soul, the intellect, the egoist self and the body.

Even in modern times, this ancient mystic practice retains its identity in Kanyakumari Ashram at Sakori near Shirdi. The great philosopher saint Shri Upasani Maharaj rejuvenated this ancient tradition by bestowing the knowledge and rights for Vedic rituals on his female disciples. In the later years, the knowledge about this Yagnic tradition was propagated throughout the world by his disciple Shri Godavari Mataji.

5.3 Sudarshan Kriya (सुदर्शन क्रिया)

A *Vastu* having predominant flaws associated with its Southern direction, is subjected to the *Yama Tandava* of the solar energies. Such a house, all the time faces unforeseen and mysterious

Vastu-Dosha and Yogic Remedies

calamities. The South direction is closely associated with the tenth house of a natural horoscope. Tenth house is a *Karma Sthan* indicative of business, employment, and paternal protection. The seventh house of a horoscope is associated with marriage. As such the tenth house, because of its fourth position from the marriage house, indicates conjugal bliss. Therefore, difficulties in marriage are invariably linked with deficiencies of the South direction. The Jaivik effects of the southern *Vastu-dosha* persist long after the dosha is terminated. *Sudarshan Kriya* propounded by the great philosopher and Yogi of modern era, Shri Shri Ravishanker is very effective in countering ill effects of *Vastu-dosha* in the South direction.

The *Sudarshan Kriya* procedure produces immediate observable constructive influences on the mind, the soul, the intellect, the egoist self, and the body. This initiates smooth circulation of the divine Pranik energy in the body, making it resistant to the effects of any *Vastu-dosha*. This *Yogic* practice includes the fundamentals of *Dhyan, Pranayama, Soham Sadhana,* and *Patanjali Yoga*. The *Nadi Shodhan* as proposed by Shri Adi Shankaracharya is easily achieved in this Kriya. In the *Japdhyan Kriya*, after chanting 1,00,000 counts (पुरश्चरण) the Jap takes microscopic form in its traverse from the *Vaikhari* to *Nabhi*. But, in Sudarshan Kriya the *Japdhyan* accelerates towards the Nabhi Chakra, as the rhythmic pace of the Prana in a sense merges the three states - Mana, Pavan, and Gagan. In such a state, the Sadhak may immediately undergo experiences like stillness of mind, unconsciousness, deep Yogic sleep, recollection of previous birth, or extreme sense of happiness. Generally, this process simulates the action of *Pingala Pranayama*, and as such, it is essential that the *Sadhak* rests himself on the right side of his body after the main *Kriya* to set the *Ida* current in motion before terminating the *Kriya*.

Vastushastra and *Yogashastra* are closely connected with the Northeast and the Southwest directions through Ida and *Pingala* current flow characteristics. Therefore, the *Sudarshan Kriya*, which simulates *Pingala Pranayama*, is one of the best antidotes against polluted *South direction*.

5.4 Shaktipat Yoga Diksha (शक्तीपात योग दिक्षा) and Reiki (रेकी)

For the *Vastu-dosha* related to the Southwest direction, it is seen that the incidents taking place in the life of the owner of the *Vastu* are closely linked with the eighth house in his horoscope. In a sense his personality is annihilated in so many ways through these events. Thinking of even a remedial measure is sometimes beyond the scope and ambit of such a person. In such cases, help indeed is available through a *Diksha* similar to *Shaktipat Diksha*, in which Pranik energy circulates through the human mind, intellect, and body under the guidance and control of a *Guru* or the Master. At appropriate time, counselling and teachings of the Guru smoothly initiate in the *Mana*, *Chitta*, and *Buddhi Koshas* of the disciple, the processes of *Kundalini Jagaran* (awakening the *Kundalini*) to *Chakrabhedan Kriya* (passage through the Chakras). Maharashtra is blessed with outstanding Saint figures with powers to channelise Pranik energy flow through *Shaktipat Diksha* — Shri Gulavani Maharaj and Shri Muktananda in the immediate past, and Shri Malharibaba of Chandrapur, and Shri Chitvilasnanda of Vajreshwari in the present era. They have been using these powers in a constructive manner. The thoughts and wishes of the *Satguru* can automatically catalyse many a *Yogic Kriya* in the disciple to ease the circulation of the *Pranik* energy flow and smoothening of the difficult tasks like *Yama-Niyama*.

Reiki a Japanese meditation practice is very popular nowadays. *Reiki* can also be classified as a type of *Shaktipat Yoga*. *Reiki* involves circulation of *motherly tender touch*, mother and *child dialogue*, and motherly yogic processes in the *Mana*, *Chitta*, and *Buddhi Koshas* of the *Sadhak* to take him to a higher dimension of consciousness. In *Reiki* treatment, positive thoughts and wishes of a person and his mental attitude brings about flow of cosmic energy through the *Panch-koshas* of the patient or the personality suffering difficulties in life. It is possible to simulate *Reiki*-like Yoganidra type energy channelling through the use of *Hindu* symbols like *Aum*, *Swastika*, *Lotus*, *Mantrabeej* etc.

5.5 Transcendental Meditation

Maharshi Mahesh Yogiji has developed the yogic discipline of Transcendental Meditation. This yogic line of *Sadhana* uses many a practices from the ancient *Patanjali Yoga*, interwoven with insight of modern psychology. The technique aims at achieving happiness in day to day life by managing the entire day through the precepts of yogic philosophy. For the present day stressful lifestyles governed by *hurry*, *curry*, and *worry*, this yogic style has its own importance.

Vastu-dosha associated with the West direction point towards split personality, impatient and undisciplined mental makeup. As such, Transcendental Meditation provides the right balance and discipline in routine life to counter the ill effects of deficiencies in the West direction.

5.6 Pranayama (प्राणायम) and Yogasana (योगासन)

Vastu-dosha originating from flaws in the Northwest direction generally result in disturbed mental state of the owner and the decision-making capacity of the person somehow gets neutralised by extraneous circumstances. We must note that, Northwest is controlled by the *Vayu-Tatva* (element wind) and *Pran* in fact is a manifestation of *Vayu* in the form of breath. Hence, in the Northwest type *Vastu-dosha*, the Yogasanas controlling the breathing and Pran are very important. As it is, *Yogasanas* and *Pranayama* are closely interwoven. Regular practice of *Yogasanas* makes a person aware of the sensation of Pran in the vicinity of the *Nabhi-Chakra*. *Nabhi* is also known as the dormant brain. *Nabhi*, in fact, is a source of all the energy forms in the body. The movement of Pran towards the remote *Nabhi-Chakra* proves a constructive influence on the *Mana*, *Chitta*, and *Buddhi*. This rejuvenating and invigorating Yogashakti can overcome all types of *doshas* or drawbacks in life.

Even the Chinese Yogic philosophy considers *Nabhi-Pranayam* (नाभी प्राणायम) as an important aspect of *Yogic* practice. Breathing technique of infants and young children involves in and out movement of stomach. The relevance of this natural movement in inhalation and exhalation, and in general, for deep and sustained breathing is well understood in Chinese Yogic practice.

In the Indian Astang Yoga (अष्टांग योग), the Asanas (आसन), body postures and rhythmic movement of the body automatically inculcate the deep breathing techniques in the *Sadhak*.

5.7 Vipasana (विपासना)

Vipasana is basically a Dhyan technique derived from *Buddha Dharma* practices. It is similar to the *Neti-Neti* (नेती नेती), *Tratak* (त्राटक), Bhrumadhya (भ्रूमध्य), and other Dhyan procedures in Indian Yogashastra. The essence of *Vipasana* practice lies in achieving the *Turiya* (तुरीया), the fourth state of consciousness by remaining inactive witness (साक्षीभाव) to the transitions taking place in the surroundings. *Turiya* is a state of mind beyond Jagruti (जागृती), *Swapna* (स्वप्न), and Sushupti (सुषुप्ती), but at microscopic level its presence is noted in all the three states. Vipasana takes the Sadhak towards *Turiya* through Layayog (लययोग) and Swaryog (स्वरयोग).

Vastu-dosha in the North direction generally implies heart troubles. This direction is associated with the fourth house in a horoscope, and with *Jaivik Urja* in *Vastushastra*.

In the Chinese acupuncture technique, it is assumed that the energy contours for senses define circular Chakra type path in the body. In *Vipasana* concentrated power of the mind is focused on various *Bindus* or points in the body and on different parts of the body in a sequential manner. Acupuncture technique aims at inducing revitalising vibrations in biochemical processes by applying pressure on specific points on *Chakra*-shaped energy contours. Similar effect is achieved in *Vipasana* by making use of subtle energies of mind and senses in the process of meditation.

Taking up a role of a non-interacting witness, constantly watching the inner and outer movements of the breathing process is the backbone of *Vipasana* technique. The experience can best be described in words of Sant Dyaneshwar: मनासी टाकीले मागे। गतीशी तुळणा नसे ।। (its speed is simply incomparable, it has even

Vastu-Dosha and Yogic Remedies

outpaced the mind itself). The *Dhyan* technique of observing the self by becoming inactive witness finds references in *Nath-Pantha* (नाथपंथ) sect also. The sect in fact describes the all encompassing Vipasana through the couplets like;

|| अलख निरंजन || (*Jap recitation*),
|| दिनभर ऐसे नजरभर देखे वही पुरुष निर्मोही || (*Gorakh song*),
|| निरखिरा निरखिरा गेली ये वो || (*Sant Dyaneshwar*).

Yogashastra postulates: || जेथे मन तेथे प्राणशक्ती || (life-force is located at the point where the mind is focused). *Layayog* and its spherical vibrations of sensation cleanse the entire body by attaining the necessary concentration of mind.

5.8 Soham Sadhana (सोऽहम् साधना)

Soham Sadhana incorporates *Sadhana* techniques like *Pranayama* (प्राणायम), *Swaryog* (स्वरयोग), *Tratak* (त्राटक), *Sakshibhav* (साक्षीभाव), *Pranav Sadhana* (प्रणव साधना), and *Sudarshan Kriya* (सुदर्शन क्रिया). It is basically the *Rajyoga Diksha* (राजयोग दीक्षा) prescribed by the Nath sect. This Sadhana has a set pattern - *Bhasrika* (भस्त्रीका), *Aumkar Uccharan* (ॐकार उच्चारण), *Ujjayi Shwasan* (उज्जयी श्वसन), and then constant observation of the self without active participation. By watching the slow moving rhythm of the breathing process, the mind is brought under control. *Soham Sadhana* is the art of experiencing the formless *Gagan* and imbibing its essence by making the *Mana* (mind) ride the chariot of *Pavan*.

This *Dhyan* technique is most effective on the *Vastu-dosha* associated with Northeast direction, which affects the sources of positive energy flow. The Northeast directional deficiencies produce detrimental effects matching in intensity to those originating from the *Vastu-dosha* in the Southwest direction. As such, *Soham Sadhana*, which derives its strength from all the *Yoga* disciplines is beneficial as a remedy against *Vastu-dosha* in the Northeast direction.

Soham Sadhana vanquishes the *Doshas* related to the four basic elements - *Prithvi*, *Aap*, *Tej*, and *Vayu* - by focusing sublime qualities of the element *Gagan* on the mind.

Bhasrika removes the bad habits like laziness and sleepiness in the Sadhak, facilitating *Nadi-Shodhan* (refining the Nadi). *Pranav-Ucchar* awakens the senses in the deep confines of the inner *Pran-Kosha*. *Ujjayi Shwasan* creates a link between natural Soham reaction and the individual breathing process. This in turn constructs a bridge to *Pinda-Brahma*, which is essential for smooth passage of the *Pran Shakti*. Then, the dormant *Mana* (mind) can easily ascend to the *Gagan*.

Since *Soham Sadhana* is a ritual suited for *Rajyoga*, it is smooth, easy, and safe. In Maharashtra this *Sadhana* has been rejuvenated through the efforts of Shri Swarupananda, Shri Madhavnath, and Shri Yoginitai.

This chapter discussed the relevance of different yogic practices for pacifying the mind and body subjected to ill effects brought about by flaws in qualities of *Vastu* directions. The benefits of the above yogic disciplines are manifold. An individual not only achieves stability of mind and mental peace, his body and mind develop the strength to successfully counter the ill effects of direction related *Vastu-dosha*. Thus, he is blessed with a cosmic protective shield.

6. ASTROLOGY IN VASTU ANALYSIS

6.1 Astrology and Vastushastra
Foundations of Astrology and *Vastushastra* can be traced to the concept of five great elements. As a corollary to this factor, it is natural to find similarity and harmony between the horoscope of an individual and the *Vastu* situation encountered by him.

Vibrations, waves, sound, and light are the four basic parameters involved in defining the state and character of a house. As astrological studies also involve these four factors, an interesting interrelationship between Astrology and *Vastushastra* can be observed. Vibrations, waves, sound, and light influence the environment of a house, making it either holy or impure. Wherever necessary, rectification is possible through improvement of vibrations of the various directions.

The remedial measures against *Vastu-dosha* (misplaced stream in a house) include compensation through additional vibrations, rectification through extra waves, reinforcement of existing waves through primordial sound, and purification by rightly guided direction of flow of light. The four different tools utilised for this purpose are;
1. Colours
2. Plants (naturally growing and bonsai)
3. Chanting of classical '*Mantras*' along with '*Yagna*'
4. Regulating the solar radiation flow in the house.

Since these instruments for changes in *Vastu* environment do not involve any demolition or structural alterations, these are quite effective and eminently suited for apartments or flats not constructed as per *Vastu* techniques.

One of the popular charts from the astrological almanacs or ephemera is the '*Avak-Hada-Chakra*' which helps in improving the Vastu environment by using the above tools. This chart is a

The Avak-Hada Chakra

Rasi (Zodiac)	Nakshatra (Constellation)	Aradhya Vriksha (Benevolent Tree)	Panch-Maha-Bhuta (Element)
Mesha (Aries)	Ashwini Bharani Kritika	Kuchla Awali Umber	Air Fire Fire
Vrishabh (Taurus)	Kritika 2, 3, 4 Rohini Mriga 1, 2	Umber Jambhli Khair	Fire Earth Air
Mithun (Gemini)	Mriga 3, 4 Ardra Punarvasu 1, 2, 3	Khair Krishnagaru Velu	Air Water Air
Karka (Cancer)	Punarvasu 4 Pushya Aslesha	Velu Pimpal Nagchafa	Air Fire Water
Simha (Leo)	Magha Purva Uttara 1, 2	Vat Palas Dhayari	Fire Fire Air
Kanya (Virgo)	Uttara 3, 4 Hastha Chitra 1, 2	Dhayari Jayi Bel	Air Air Air
Tula (Libra)	Chitra 3, 4 Swati Vishakha 1, 2, 3	Bel Arjun Nagkeshar	Air Fire Earth
Vruschik (Scorpio)	Vishakha 4 Anuradha Jyeshtha	Nagkeshar Nagkeshar Samber	Earth Earth Earth
Dhanu (Sagittarius)	Moola Purvashadha Uttarashadha 1	Ral Vet Phanas	Water Water Earth
Makar (Capricorn)	Uttarashadha 2, 3, 4 Shravan Dhanishtha 1, 2	Phanas Rui Shami	Earth Earth Earth

Contd...

Contd...

Kumbha (Aquarius)	Dhanishtha 3, 4 Shatataraka Purvabhadrapada 1, 2, 3	Shami Shami Kalamb	Earth Earth Fire
Meena (Pisces)	Purvabhadrapada 4 Uttarabhadrapada Revati	Amra Kadulimb Moha	Fire Water Water

Table 6.1: Constellations, great elements, and benevolent trees

magical wand that correlates directions, *Nakshatra* (constellation), colours, numerology, plant-kingdom, and the five great elements. It shows the way for achieving divine correlation between a tiny house and the gigantic cosmos, using the simplest possible techniques.

Amra (Mangifera indica)
Bel (Aegle marmelos)
Jayi (Jasmin auriculata)
Kalamb (Anthoceph.cadamba)
Kuchla (Strychnon nux-vomica)
Palas (Butea monosperma)
Ral (Shorea robusta)
Shami (Prosopis spicigera)
Velu (Dendro. stricts)

Arjun (Terminalia arjuna)
Dhayari (Buxus sempe.)
Kadulimb (Azadiracta indica)
Khair (Prosopis cinerama)
Moha (Madhuca lati.)
Phanas (Jackfruit tree)
Rui (Gossypium arbo.)
Umber (Ficus racemosa),
Vet (Dendro.ind.)

Awali (Emblica officinalis)
Jambhli (Syzygium cumini)

Krishnagaru (Acquilaria)
Nagkeshar (Mesua fera)
Pimpal (Ficus religiosa)
Samber (Iribuus terrestris)
Vat (Ficus bengalensis)

Chart 6.1: Generic Names for Trees in Avak-Hada Chakra

Use of *'Avak-Hada Chakra'* is of immense importance in Vastu science as it provides the most comprehensive data on interrelationship between vibrations, waves, sound, and light on one hand and colours, plants, *'Mantras'*, and solar system on the other. In this chapter, we will indicate the ways to apply this remedy in a simple manner, by considering only the *'Dev-Nakshatras'*. The Table 6.1 gives an extract from the *'Avak-Hada Chakra'* that is useful in *Vastu* science. Additionally, colours can be correlated with the *Nakshatra* type.

Vastu imbalance is essentially distortions in the energy fields aligned with the house. Rectification of these energy fields, correction of rhythm in the aligned electromagnetic flux, stabilising the ground waves in the vicinity of the house and regulating the solar flux are some of the methods used for countering any *Vastu-dosha*.

Earth, water, wind, fire, and ether are the five great elements with more refined micro level of expression from one element to the next. But, as far as macro parameters like energy and existence are concerned, it is an ascending order from the earth element to the ether element. The five qualities associated with the five great elements - sound, touch, form, taste, and smell - can be used for classifying activity spectrum of the elements.

	SOUND	TOUCH	FORM	TASTE	SMELL	QUALITIES
EARTH	YES	YES	YES	YES	YES	5
WATER	YES	YES	NO	YES	YES	4
WIND	YES	YES	NO	NO	YES	3
FIRE	YES	YES	NO	NO	NO	2
ETHER	YES	NO	NO	NO	NO	1

Table 6.2: Qualities of five great elements

From the chart we can infer that 'finer the element, lesser is the degree of expression, but higher is the degree of efficiency'. The intelligent way to improve a *Vastu* is to use the subtle and finer great elements as catalysts. Earth has a limited effect on water, water has limited effect on wind, wind has limited effect on fire etc. But, as far as power and energy are concerned, fire is more effective than wind, wind effective than water etc. For everlasting effects, it is prudent to use finer and micro level elements, which are more effective in bringing about changes in the environment of a house.

Using remedies from '*Avak-Hada Chakra*' is a subtle way for deep and lasting effects. A house can attain 'cosmic envelope' - order and bliss of nature - by linking the inner micro fields to outer space macro fields through the techniques of *Vastu* science.

Every energy field has associated with itself characteristic field quanta or exchange particles that mediate transmission of force. The mass-energy equivalence principle can be used to assess the energy or mass of the particle, if one of the parameters is known. Quanta with zero mass can act at infinite distance i.e. graviton in gravitation field and photon in electromagnetic field. The Eastern concepts of 'aura', 'radiance' and the term of recent origin 'bio-energy-field' refer to specific energy fields associated with living organisms in general and human beings in particular.

The Eastern mythological thought processes believe that the evolution of living beings can be visualised in terms of subtle and finer energy fields that are aligned with any given individual. It is said that the *'Panch-koshas'* (five vessels or cores) are expressions of five great elements. The expression of the five great elements in an individual and contribution of qualities by these elements to an individual personality varies as per the *Prarabdha* or *Poorva-Sanskara* (pre-ordained situation or outcome of an earlier birth). This makes every individual a singular personality. The inner or micro-space of an individual is a unique combination of the five great elements together with the *Poorva-Sanskara*.

In *Vastu* science, we correlate the micro-space to macro-space, inner space to outer space through a kind of harmony and rhythm in the energy fields. In the cosmic envelope attained by a *Vastu*, the *Prarabdha* or *Poorva-Sanskara* undergoes qualitative changes. One who lives in the properly attained cosmic envelope of a *Vastu* enters an energy field where there is no friction, impedance, or loss of energy. He also breaks the previous frames of reference and each of the cells and particles of his organic being experiences enriched, blissful environment. These miraculous results are possible through changes made as per *Vastushastra* rules.

Vastushastra remedies is an aesthetic combination of various techniques to channelise and polarise the multiple fine spectra of cosmic energies. It is a well-known fact from biophysics and biochemistry that polarised light has specific effect on bio-chemical and organic processes. Bio-chemical processes generally involve ionic exchange, i.e., flow of ions across a membrane. The external rhythmic polarised energy in tune with the internal organic elements in a body easily gets absorbed in the organic entity. This fresh breath of energy at organic cellular level is endowed with power to erase the old reference frames of a cell. A cell thus transformed acts as a new cell with additional sources of power and energy. In a way, this is rebirth for the organic substance, or in religious terminology, the '*Poorva-Sanskara*' of a cell or an organism is removed and bondage of '*Prarabdha*' ceases to exist.

In *Yogashastra*, the same results are achieved by regulating the flow of '*Prana*' and polarising the *Pranik* energy on the mind and conscious, to provide a new frame of reference at bio-chemical level, which leads to freedom and ever-flowing happiness for the individual.

6.2 Horoscope and Vastu-dosha

Planetary position at birth defines the position of an individual in a cosmic energy network. *Vastushastra* also creates an energy network, which overcomes the effects of planetary positions. In a sense, Vastushastra provides the most powerful remedy to reduce the *Poorva-Sanskara* effects. Taking recourse to modern concepts, we can say that forces generated out of *Vastushastra* remedy decode and nullify the old quantum memory associated with the human mind and create a cosmic envelope around the human vessel through harmony, rhythm, and polarisation.

Directional faults in the house occupied by a person and *Vastu-dosha* are directly related to his horoscope. After detailed study of numerous horoscopes, certain inferences can be drawn out to diagnose *Vastu-dosha* from any given horoscope. We are indicating here the rules that have to be followed for such an analysis. Case studies have also been presented to prove the effectiveness of this method.

6.2.1 Basic Assumptions in Horoscope Analysis

For interpreting a horoscope in *Vastu* terms, certain guidelines are necessary. We are giving here some basic rules, which are very useful in *Astro-Vastu* analysis. Experienced astrologers can derive other subtle rules applicable to Vastu situations, based on this logical pattern.

Astrology in Vastu Analysis 51

Ten Rules
1. Powerful position of the first house owner in a horoscope indicates that the *Vastu* is having good ventilation and entry or openings are from the East direction. Hence, both the person and the *Vastu* can be predicted to be benefiting from qualities relating to intelligence, personality, social status, and physical form.
2. Saturn in the 7th house indicates that it is powerful as far as its directional status is concerned. The Saturn in the 7th house bestows a full-moon-day effect on the planets in the 1st house. Naturally, planets in the first house with their ownership over specific houses and directions will have good effects, both for the horoscope and the *Vastu*. A person with such a horoscope will have slopes towards the East in his *Vastu-kshetra* (plot) and the West openings will be closed - implying good effects of the East direction for the *Vastu*. On the other hand, any evil effect of Saturn on the first house lead to the following inferences - West entry for the *Vastu*, ventilation from the West, staircase and/or toilets in the East, the East direction completely blocked etc.
3. Presence of '*Papgraha*' in the 4th house and incorrect position of owner of the 4th house indicates that the *Vastu* of such a person may have the following deficiencies;
   * toilets to the North,
   * staircase to the North,
   * blocked North direction,
   * entry from the South direction,
   * house with North-South axis shorter than East-West axis.
4. Owner of the 1st house in the 12th, 8th, or the 6th house implies that map axis will not match with the geometric axis of the house.
5. Owner of the 7th house placed in the 6th or 12th house and inauspicious planetary position for the 7th house is indicative of the following flaws in the *Vastu*;
   * underground water tank located in the West zone,

* ground slopes towards the West,
* open terraces on the West side,
* blocked East direction,
* entrance from the West,
* substantial ventilation from the West direction.

6. Owner of the 10th house in undesired position and 10th house clubbed with incorrect planetary positions preordain the following *Vastu-doshas*;
   * either the plot or the construction is of '*Vyaghra-Mukh*' type,
   * excessive low levels on the South and Southwest sides,
   * more side margins on the South side,
   * entrance from the South direction,
   * distortions in the qualities of the North direction.
7. Incorrect placement of Moon and its association with '*Papgraha*' indicates misplaced North of the Vastu.
8. Incorrect location of Sun subjected to attack by Saturn spells severe *Vastu-dosha* in the South direction.
9. '*Kal-sarpa*' horoscope may point towards various Vastu-doshas with severe consequences.
10. Comparing the characteristics of a *Vastu* and horoscope of the dweller is one of the better means to judge the accuracy of a given horoscope.

6.2.2 The Planetary Relationships

There is a definite correlation between the zodiac signs and the ruling planets of these signs. The degree of inter-planetary friendship or enmity originates from the characteristics of five great elements, which are associated with various constellations and planets. The three tables displayed here give summary of these relationships in terms of zodiac signs and directions governed or influenced by the planets.

Astrology in Vastu Analysis 53

Lord Planet of Zodiac Sign	Zodiac Sign (Direction)	Constellations of Zodiac	Characteristic Element
Mars	Aries (East)	Ashwini Bharani Kritika	Fire
Venus	Taurus (Northeast)	Kritika 2, 3, 4 Rohini Mriga 1, 2	Earth
Mercury	Gemini (Northeast)	Mriga 3, 4 Ardra Punarvasu 1, 2, 3	Wind
Moon	Cancer (North)	Punarvasu 4 Pushya Aslesha	Water
Sun	Leo (Northwest)	Magha Purva Uttara 1, 2	Fire
Mercury	Virgo (Northwest)	Uttara 3, 4 Hastha Chitra 1, 2	Earth
Venus	Libra (West)	Chitra 3, 4 Swati Vishakha 1, 2, 3	Wind
Mars	Scorpio (Southwest)	Vishakha 4 Anuradha Jyeshtha	Water
Jupiter	Sagittarius (Southwest)	Moola Purvashadha Uttarashadha 1	Fire
Saturn	Capricorn (South)	Uttarashadha 2, 3, 4 Shravan Dhanishtha 1, 2	Earth
Saturn	Aquarius (Southeast)	Dhanishtha 3, 4 Shatataraka Purvabhadrapada 1, 2, 3	Wind
Jupiter	Pisces (Southeast)	Purvabhadrapada 4 Uttarabhadrapada Revati	Water

Table 6.3: Lord Planets - Zodiac Signs - Five Great Elements

The rules detailed in this chapter result from comprehensive study of these characteristics. *Nakshatras* or constellations are assigned specific *Panch-Maha-Bhuta* characteristics. These qualities are reflected in the corresponding zodiac sign. In a horoscope, the planets rule over certain directions, while the zodiac signs have their own directional domains of influence. All these factors present an interesting prospect of multiple permutations and combinations.

Characteristic Element for the Direction	Direction	Planetary Lord of the Direction
Fire (Agni)	East (Poorva)	Sun (Ravi)
Wind (Vayu)	Northwest (Vayavya)	Moon (Chandra)
Earth (Prithvi)	South (Dakshin)	Mars (Mangal)
Ether (Akash)	North (Uttar)	Mercury (Budha)
Water (Jal)	Northeast (Ishanya)	Jupiter (Guru)
		Dragon Tail (Ketu)
Fire (Agni)	Southeast (Agneya)	Venus (Shukra)
Water (Jal)	West (Paschim)	Saturn (Shani)
Earth (Prithvi)	Southwest (Nairutya)	Dragon Head (Rahu)

Table 6.4: Directions and Planets in Astrology

Planet	Friend	Neutral	Enemy
SUN	Moon Mars Jupiter	Mercury	Venus Saturn Rahu
MOON	Sun Mercury	Mars Jupiter Venus Saturn	Rahu
MARS	Sun Moon Jupiter	Venus Saturn	Mercury Rahu
MERCURY	Sun Venus Saturn	Mars Jupiter Rahu	Moon
JUPITER	Sun Moon Mars	Saturn Rahu	Mercury Venus
VENUS	Mercury Saturn Rahu	Mars Jupiter	Sun Moon
SATURN	Venus Mercury Rahu	Jupiter	Sun Moon Mars

Table 6.5: Astrological Relationship between Planets

Astrology in Vastu Analysis 55

6.3 Vastu-dosha and Cyclic Repetition
A correlation can be noticed between a specific *Vastu-dosha* and cyclic repetition of grievances, sorrows, and inclement conditions.

* If the *Vastu-dosha* is related to the East, the North, or the West directions, then non-recoverable loss in small instalments is foreseen due to the short cycles and periods of Mars influencing the East, Moon the North, and Venus the West direction. The repetition of difficulties follows the Mars cycle of 45 days, Moon cycle of 2.25 days, or Venus cycle of 28 days.
* If the Vastu-dosha is in the South direction, then some fatal incidents are forecast every 12 years or 25 years. Saturn rules the South direction with a long cycle of 27 years. Such Saturn shocks due to *Vastu-dosha* in the South zone radically change a person's pattern of life on account of heavy losses.
* *Vastu-dosha* in the Northeast or Northwest indicates slow, steady, and sustained effects on the entire family due to short cycles of the Sun, Venus and Mercury.
* *Vastu-dosha* in the Southwest and Southeast gives worst effects with repetition of events every 13th and 25th year. Jupiter transits through the Southwest direction with a cycle of 13 years, and Saturn controls Southeast direction over a long cycle of 27 years. As per *Vastu-Purush-Mandal*, the deities associated with South, Southwest and Southeast directions - *Yama, Agni,* and *Niruta* — are pointers to this aspect.

6.4 Analytical Case
Here, we are presenting a specific example wherein the horoscope of the owner of a *Vastu* was analysed to understand the characteristic flaws and virtues of the *Vastu* he was dwelling in. Site visit was then arranged to compare these predicted trends with the actual properties of the *Vastu*. It was found that the *Vastu-doshas* were a reflection of the flaws in planetary positions in horoscope of the owner.

In this particular case, the specific *Vastu* situation has been analysed from astrological as well *Vastushastra* point of view to find practical remedies that can provide relief to the dweller, and help him in overcoming difficulties in life.

Client: Mr. ABC

Site Location: Near Boat Club, Pune

Prelude: The name *Vastushastra* signifies it to be a science of forces. Though it may appear to be mundane and unfathomable, it should not be considered vague or ambiguous. All the rules and regulations of *Vastushastra* can be understood in terms of electromagnetism, gravity, light, radiation, cosmic rays, particle physics and related topics. Hence the rules of *Vastushastra* must be followed with due care and attention.

Site Analysis:
1. Since the building lies in the East and the Southeast zone, disturbances are created in every righteous action, leading to unrest in everyday activities.
   * To activate the East stream and to increase the East flow, glossy colours should be provided on the East walls.
   * The West margin should be reduced to about 1.5 meter from the building by constructing a stone wall.
   * Landscaping should raise the ground level on the West Side. Neem and Nilgiri trees should be planted alternately in the raised plateau.
2. Toilets in the Northeast and East zone indicate family problems and loss of communication between family members staying in the house.
   * In such a case, toilets in the Northeast zone should be removed and a large window should be provided in the Northeast to activate the Northeast as the source direction.
3. Ventilation from the South implies that the Pranik and the *Jaivik Urja* are in mutually opposite directions leading to waste of organic energy and the life force.
   * The effective remedy here is to provide tilt-bay windows for simulating East stream at the South window location.

4. '*Vyaghra-Mukh*' or tiger faced building form with width of South side more than the width of North side indicates loss of younger members of the family and health problems for the young ones.
    * The tiger form effect can be removed and geometric rhythm achieved by providing 'Pergola' enclosure at the roof level by locating one circular column in the Northwest corner.
5. Anti-clockwise staircase disturbs the natural cyclic rhythm of the mind, body and intellect.
    * The anti-clockwise rhythm can be broken by through symbols - carving of clockwise arrow design on each step.
6. The underground water tank in the Southeast zone works against the natural position of element 'Fire' and resulting in impediments to Jaivik Urja flow.
    * Here, the underground water tank should be removed from the Southeast zone and placed in the Northeast zone.
7. Extended West margins in the plot indicate problems in partnership, differences in marital relations and failure or loss of fortune in prolonged court battle. This is also reflected in the 7th house planetary position in the natural horoscope.
    * Construction of compound wall and landscaping of the West zone to achieve proper balance as indicated in item (1) can offset this problem.
8. Southwest entrance to the plot represents accident-prone environment and forewarns unhappiness resulting from activities of spouse and/or the next generation. '*Vithi-Shula*' (dead-end) from the Southwest reinforces the above argument.
    To eradicate negative elements of the Southwest entry and the dead-end effect, a pyramid should be provided over the Southwest entry zone.
9. To match the shape, size and periphery of the '*Vastu-kshetra*' with the 'helix' form, variations in depth, height, and widths should be attempted in landscaping. The

helical alignment in landscaping equalises the vices and virtues related to the directions and sub-directions.

10. Planting of trees based on '*Vruksha-Vichar*' is a well-defined concept in Vastu analysis. There appears to be a close affinity between plants and human beings, a relationship that goes beyond sharing of biosphere and chemical substances.

   * Trees should be planted all around the periphery of the property as per the details indicated below.
   * In case the tree sample indicated in chart is not available, a tree from the same family may be planted to achieve similar, if not identical results.

Direction	Tree
East	Kuchla
Northeast	Khair, Velu
North	Pimpal
Northwest	Jayee
West	Arjun
Southwest	Nagkeshar
South	Rui
Southeast	Moha

   * In addition to these, Audumber and Neem trees should be planted on the South side to provide humid environment, and to enrich the environment through temperature reduction. Medicinal shrubs/plants and Nilgiri trees should be located on the West side. Since the West and Northwest are the zones of the basic element '*Vayu*', aroma of these plants and bliss as per the '*Vruksha-Vichar*' will spread throughout the *Vastu*.

11. Presence of a big river on the North side has qualities to alleviate most of the difficulties discussed here. Still, 30% to 40% of the difficult conditions are bound to exert their influence, which is to be reduced through the other remedial measures indicated above.

Here, the site was analysed from *Vastushastra* point of view to choose effective remedial measures. In the next chapter on '*Vastu-Jyotisha*' more cases have been discussed to gain further insight into relevance of astrology in analysing *Vastu-dosha* and *Vastu* situation.

7. VASTU - JYOTISHA

Human body is enfolds the '*Manas*' or the mind. As per Hindu religious tenets, man's existence is based on *Panch-koshas*. A house is nothing but a manifestation of outer *Kosha* of the man. The formation of *Panch-koshas* in a man and the house he builds depend on the *Prarabdha* (fate), *Niyati* (destiny), and *Purva-sanskar* (apriori proclivities). We can therefore find compatibility between the astrological horoscope and the *Vastushastra* horoscope.

Resemblance of the human body with a house has been a topic of interest in many a religious discourses by saints and yogis. Similarity of body and house is projected in such discussions. The affinity of the mind and the body on one hand, between the mind and the house on the other are parallel concepts. This analogy is seen in many couplets like;

देह देवाचे मंदीर
कोणाचा हा देह कोणाचे हे घर
नवदरवाजे दहावी खिडकी

The comparison of a house with the human body as in religious writings, the astrological significance of the fourth house which influences heart and the house, and astrological rendition of a *Vastu* through *Vastu-Jyotisha* - all these factors have a common platform. Here, we have tried to analyse some personal horoscopes to speculate the nature of the *Vastu*, the *Vastu-doshas* and remedial measures on one hand, and enhancement of virtues of a Vastu through the broader perspective of *Vastu-Jyotisha*.

7.1 Vastu-Jyotish Case Studies
Analysis (1)

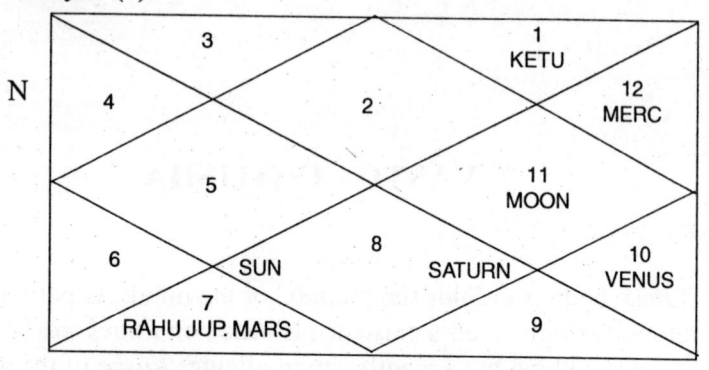

```
         3              1
                        KETU
N   4         2              12
                             MERC
       5              11
                      MOON
    6        8
       SUN      SATURN    10
       7                  VENUS
    RAHU JUP. MARS    9
```

Fig.7.1: Horoscope for analytical case (1)

1. Sun the lord of the fourth house is placed in the seventh house in conjunction with the Saturn. Since the fourth house is a pointer towards the North direction, flaws in the fourth house will show up as deficiency in the North zone of the *Vastu*. These deficiencies pertain to massiveness of the North or blocked North direction in the Vastu.

   On inspection, the entire Vastu is found to be located in the North zone, with the staircase placed on the North side of the Vastu.

2. Lord of the seventh house Mars placed in the sixth house in union with Jupiter and Rahu and Saturn in the seventh house in union with the Sun. This implies a flaw in the West direction of the *Vastu*. As per *Vastushastra*, the deficiency in the West zone is indicated through the following parameters - entrance in the West, more openings towards the West, slopes towards the West, excess margin on the West side, or a deep pit in the West zone.

   On inspection, the house in fact, was found to have West Side entrance, a vacant plot adjacent to the house on the West side, and a borewell in the West zone.

3. A '*Kal-Sarpa-Yog*' in a horoscope is indicative of mismatched directions for the *Vastu* or the *Vastu* located at the dead-end of a road. As in '*Kal-Sarpa-Yog*', where no

Vastu-Jyotisha

planet can exert its influence, the *Vastu* is subjected to evil effects of dead-end situation and mismatch of directions.
4. The position of the Lord of the tenth house indicates flaw in the Southern zone, as confirmed by a vacant playground of a school placed on the South side of the *Vastu*.

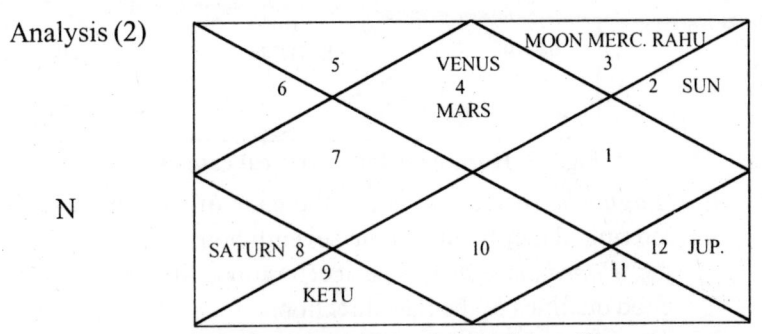

Analysis (2)

```
                5       MOON MERC. RAHU
           6        VENUS      3
                      4              2   SUN
                    MARS
                7                  1

   SATURN 8          10         12  JUP.
              9                11
           KETU
```

N

Fig.7.2: Horoscope for analytical case (2)

1. Lord of the fourth house in '*Lagna*', and also in auspicious line of sight of Jupiter and Saturn. Lord of the fifth house and Lord of the tenth house in union in a *Jala-Rashi*. All these factors point towards qualitative virtues of the North direction
2. Debilitated '*Lagnesh*', Mercury trapped by Rahu and ineffective Mars in '*Lagna*' indicate flaw in the East direction.
3. The Sun in the eleventh house under the gaze of Saturn and in the twelfth '*Vyaya-Sthan*' union of the Moon, Rahu, and Mercury indicate major flaw in the Southeast direction.
4. The polluted '*Dhanesh*' and Lord of the third house point towards flaws in the Northeast direction.

Situation:
1. River with an uninterrupted flow on the North side, and the plot sloping towards the North.
2. The Vastu has a minimum of margin on the East Side.
3. Dead-end on the Southeast side and water-tank in the Southeast zone.
4. Toilets on the Northeast side.

Analysis (3)

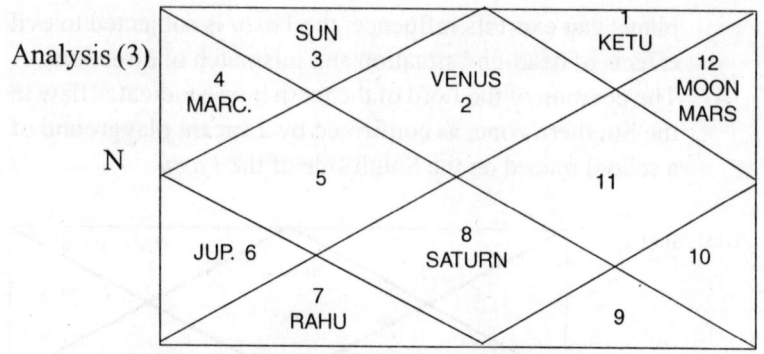

N

```
         SUN
          3
   4            VENUS     KETU
 MARC.            2        1
                                  12
                                MOON
                                MARS
          5             11

                  8
 JUP. 6       SATURN             10
          7
         RAHU           9
```

Fig.7.3: Horoscope for analytical case (3)

1. *'Lagnesh'* strong and under the gaze of Jupiter. A slow moving planet Saturn in the seventh house, giving Venus the *'Poornima-effect'* type acceleration. All these nurture good qualities of the East direction.
2. The Saturn in the seventh house is its own zone, and it is also the 'Bhagyesh' - indicating absence of flaws in the West direction.
3. Jupiter in *Kanya Rashi* and Saturn in Scorpion i.e. debilitated lords of the eighth and ninth house point towards major flaws in the Southwest direction.
4. Moon in the Pisces in union with Mars and under the gaze of Jupiter show absence of flaws in the Southeast direction.

Situation:
1. Entrance on the East Side and open spaces in that direction.
2. The West Side completely blocked.
3. Truncated Southwest zone.
4. Kitchen located in the Southeast zone.

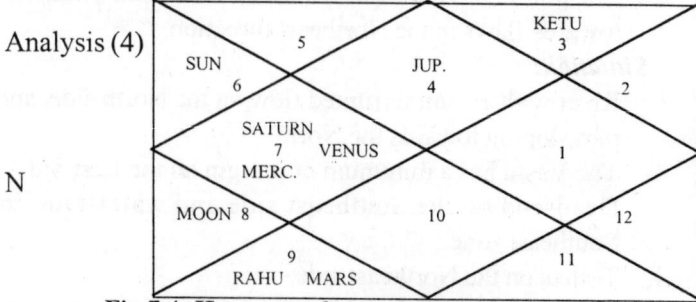

Analysis (4)

N

```
              5
   SUN              JUP.      KETU
    6                4          3
                                     2
   SATURN
     7      VENUS
    MERC.                     1
   MOON 8            10            12
         9                    11
        RAHU  MARS
```

Fig.7.4: Horoscope for analytical case (4)

Vastu-Jyotisha

1. Jupiter, the *Bhagyesh* in *Lagna* in strength. *Lagnesh* in the fifth house under the gaze of Jupiter. These indicate good qualities for the East direction.
2. Strong Saturn in the fourth house in union with friendly planets and Venus (Lord of the fourth house) in its own house indicate positive qualities of the North direction.
3. The Moon in Scorpion, evil conjugation of Saturn and Mars, Mars-Rahu union in the sixth house indicates flaws in the Northwest direction.
4. Mars (Lord of the tenth house) placed in the sixth house in union with Rahu and under the gaze of Saturn, point towards flaws in the South direction.

Situation:
1. Entrance on the East Side, maximum windows and openings on that side.
2. The North-South length of the house is more than the East-West width.
3. Excess Northwest side.
4. Due to the tin roofing of the shanties on the South side, excess solar heat from the South side.

7.2 Chandranadi, Suryanadi, and Vastu-Jyotisha

Time flows like a river, and you cannot twice step into the same river. Every human being has different rhythms of body, mind, and intellect, distinct from those found in other individuals. As such, ripples of dissimilar nature are formed in independent individuals exposed to similar natural environment and circumstances. The basic building plans of a *Vastu* may be identical, but the constituents of an individual's life and the envelope of *Vastu* create diversity in stream of time. The overall strength in resisting *Vastu-dosha* differs from person to person. *Vastu* experts have to diagnose and build a holistic environment for an individual, keeping in mind the above-mentioned comprehensive perception about the individual.

7.2.1 Multi-storeyed Buildings - Floor Attributes

Identical plans and alignments of flats located on different floors show marked divergence of fortunes. Even the row houses having same plans and similar directional virtues demonstrate shift in fortunes. All this may be confusing for the uninitiated, but one who understands the characteristics of the moon streams and sun streams can easily bridge this gap of ignorance.

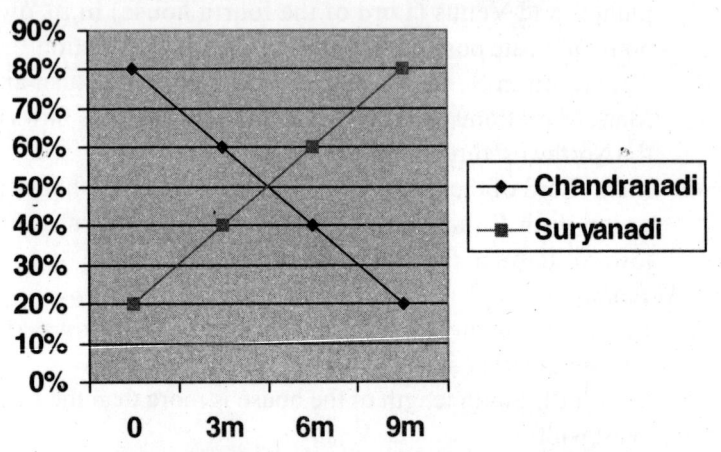

Fig. 7.5: Building Height Vs Relative Intensity of Ill-Effects due to Flaws in Moon-streams and Sun-streams

Vastu-doshas related to the North, Northeast, and East directions are flaws due to moon-streams, which are propelled by earth from ground level. Qualities or virtues related to these directions are in effect bliss sourced from moon-streams, which are projected from the sky and the sunlight. Hence, higher level floors in a multi-storeyed building will experience diminished effect of North, Northeast, and East direction flaws, and will enjoy pronounced bliss of moon streams.

Scorching sun projects sun streams responsible for *Vastu* directional faults in the South, Southeast, and Southwest. As such, *Vastu-doshas* in South, Southeast, Southwest directions will provide worst kind of effects at higher level, particularly for flats with terrace on South, Southeast, and Southwest zones and flats underneath an open terrace.

In short, the flats in the North, Northeast, and East zones of a building will have noticeable cosmic bliss on higher floors, while flats in Southwest, South, and Southeast will experience better cosmic bliss on lower floors.

7.2.2 Row Houses - Virtues of Zones

Sometimes *Vastu* experts are quite perplexed while analysing plans of row houses in a plot having apparently similar directional references.

First step in such analysis is to divide the entire row-housing complex into four sub-divisions and relate the virtues of the subdivisions with the main zone. *While evaluating Vastu aspect of a row house it is very important to know the zone in which a particular house is placed.*

	N	
ROW HOUSE 1	ROW HOUSE 2	ROW HOUSE 3
ROW HOUSE 4	ROW HOUSE 5	ROW HOUSE 6

W (left) — E (right); S (bottom)

Fig.7.6: Directionwise Zoning of Row-housing Complex

Row House No.1 lies in Northwest zone. East direction of the house is blocked and the ventilation from the North and West is confined within the limited area. The row house predominantly displays qualities of *Pavan* (wind), which is associated with flickering, unstable mind. Since this zone is under the influence of Moon, excess sentimental and passionate behaviour is foretold. This coupled with obstruction to the East direction points to life of luxury, loafing, liquor consumption, loss of character and social status. This apart, the *Vastu* will project predominant Northwest zone characteristics.

Row House No.2 lies in a zone where South and West sides are confined, with blocked East direction. This house has a stable South zone and can get uninterrupted moon streams from the North direction. Such houses are beneficial for businessmen for whom education is not the prime goal.

Row House No.3 lies in Northeast zone. Here South and West are sides are confined with North and East open. This house is best amongst all the units, as *Jaivik* flow from the North and *Pranik* flow from the East are directly available. Since zones susceptible to high thermal activity - South and West - are blocked, *Pingala* (sun stream) is completely cut-off. In general, the house will project predominant Northeast zone characteristics.

Row House Nos. 4, 5, 6 will give negative effects as moon streams from Northeast zones are obstructed and sun streams from Southwest zones are predominant. Row-house no. 4 will have Southwest zone characteristics, while house no. 6 will display Southeast zone characteristics.

From the above discussion we can infer that apparently similar plans or designs for flats or dwelling do not ensure similar *Vastu* effects. Moon-streams and sun-streams play an important role in defining the cosmic energy envelope for a *Vastu*. It is essential that each case is studied in detail and with due diligence before attempting any remedial measures on visible, hidden, or assumed *Vastu-dosha*. *Vastu*-analysis is not an isolated discipline in itself. Wherever necessary, it must look upto *Yogashastra*, Astrology, and science for necessary guidance.

8. VASTU-DOSHA AND REMEDIAL ACTION

In this chapter we will briefly outline the various paths available to mend intricate *Vastu* situations.

8.1 Vastu-dosha Analysis through Vastu-Jyotisha

As per *Vastu-Purush-Mandal*, the *Aditya* form of energy has its strength in the east direction. In astrology, the Sun in an individual horoscope is considered to be ascendant in the east direction, i.e., east is the active zone for the Sun. *Vastushastra* can serve as a key to reduce the influence of the ascendant Saturn in *Lagna*. Saturn is said to govern the west direction. Therefore, any deficiency resulting from Saturn in *Lagna* can be removed through the eastern *Aditya* current as detailed in *Vastushastra*. A person having ascendant Saturn in *Lagna* in his horoscope can build his house with east entrance, and windows and openings on the east direction to enhance the *Aditya* current and to nullify the effects of Saturn in *Lagna*.

On the other hand, for a person having the Sun in the seventh house of his horoscope the deficiency due to the displaced Sun in the 7th house can be remedied through enhancing the gravitational quality of the West direction. It is also possible to add up the positive vibrations by planting trees like Bel, Arjun, and Nagkeshar in the West direction as suited for the Saturn and the Libra zodiac as per the *Avak-Hada-Chakra*. Other remedy is to place iron rings with blue crystals in the West direction to fortify the powers of the Saturn in the West direction. Iron, as it is, provides the necessary massiveness in the West direction. If excess margins are available in the West direction of a plot (*Vastu-kshetra*), or if all the windows are placed on the West side, the shrubs and plants like Turmeric effective on Saturn flaws can be used in ritual baths to counter the deficiency in the West direction. Similarly, for the east direction flaws, the plants with Sun character say, *Lajalu* and *Manjishtha* can be used in ritual baths to remedy the situation. In Chinese Feng-Shui technique, the concept of 'Cosmic Bath' has been widely prescribed for drawing benefits from the cosmic energies.

Chinese Feng-Shui technique suggests diverse minerals to be used in bath waters for personal aura cleansing. *Gomutra* (cow urine) is traditionally used in India for purification purposes with special use of urine of a pregnant cow for deriving benefits from hormones and minerals.

A unique Hindu ritual for protecting a person from an evil eye uses crystalline rock salt for aura cleansing. Rock salt has its importance in Feng-Shui, where it is used for providing a person with protective shield against evil powers. Feng-Shui suggests that if rock salt dissolved in water is placed in vessel near a person suffering from insomnia, the air around him is purified and he goes into deep and sound sleep. For general purification and environmental cleansing, sprinkling of rock salt throughout the house is considered beneficial.

In general, a *Vastu-dosha* in any given direction is reflected in the natural horoscope through directional flaws or debilitated position of the governing planet for the direction. For example, a *Vastu-dosha* in the East direction finds corresponding flaws in the 'Dhan Sthan' (house of wealth), especially the first house. As a corollary, if the planet Sun in the horoscope is polluted, the *Vastu* is bound to have a '*dosha*' in the East direction. Similarly, a deficiency in the South direction finds corresponding flaw in the tenth house and its governing planet in the natural horoscope.

Once the correlation between the directional virtues and the relative planetary strengths is worked out, finding remedial measures becomes an easier task. A given *Vastu* with the North direction attaining virtues of the Moon, the South getting Mars characteristics, the East benefiting from qualities of the Sun, and the West receiving excellence of the Saturn can be qualitatively considered to be a good *Vastu*.

Vastu-Dosha and Remedial Action

Further, assuming position of strength for the Venus in the Southeast, the Jupiter in the Northeast, the Moon in the Northwest, and the *Rahu* in the Southwest, we can infer the direction-wise applicability of certain characteristic metals, trees, colours, and weighty substances representing these planets.

On the basis of above discussion, certain guidelines can be drawn.

* Fewer opening should be provided in the West to reflect the Saturn's contracting nature.
* Considering the fiery characteristics of the Mars, the South direction should have enhanced *'Prithvi-Tatva'* (element earth) and massiveness.
* To facilitate the Eastern *Aditya Pravah*, maximum number of windows, doors, and openings should be placed in the East.
* The North should reflect the Moon's *Jal-Tatwa* characteristic and the resultant cooling effect.

As per the *Poornima* discipline in astrology, the Moon is said to be in a charged *Poornima* (full moon) state when the Sun is in the West and the Moon is on the eastern horizon. This means, a fast moving planet achieves *Poornima* when a slow moving planet is on the western horizon and the fast moving planet is on the eastern horizon. In other words, the strength of the fast moving planet is exalted due to the extra gravitation of the slow moving planet placed 180 degrees apart. Since the Saturn rules over the West direction and is a slow moving planet, any remedial measures in the West direction to simulate Saturn characteristics gives the *Vastu* a virtuous nature. A *Vastu* can achieve divine stature if the Saturn specialities - oil, iron, massiveness, blue colour, and contraction - are reflected in the Western zone of the *Vastu*.

8.2 Directions, Planets, and Vastushastra

The importance of astrology in Vastu analysis can be traced to the fact that planetary positions determine the strength or weakness of a horoscope, and these planets have influence over directions and sub-directions, which are the governing factors in *Vastushastra*.

Vastu-dosha represents a flaw in a specific direction, and a corresponding defect in the vibrations of a particular planet. Classical lines of treatment are available in such cases to uplift the virtuous effects of a planet and to reduce negative factors to attain harmony and balance with the nature.

To regain the lost rhythm of directions, treatment for the affected planets is not only useful, it indirectly improves the aura of influence at human level. The following chart gives favourable directions of planets and the sphere of influence of the aura of a planet in various *Vastu* zones.

East	—	Sun
Northeast	—	Jupiter
North	—	Mercury
Northwest	—	Moon
West	—	Saturn
Southwest	—	Rahu
South	—	Mars
Southeast	—	Venus

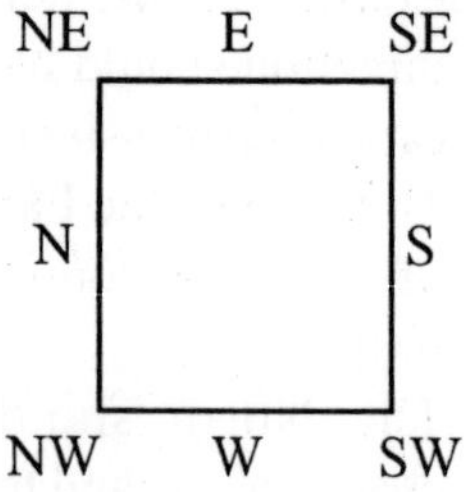

```
NE    E    SE

N          S

NW    W    SW
```

Fig.8.1: Directions and Ruling Planets

Avak-Hada-Chakra is a magical remedy for planning various corrective measures on *Vastu-dosha*, as the *Chakra* correlates colours, plants, planets, metals and classifies zodiac signs and positions under various groupings of vibrations, waves, sound, and light.

Indian astrology provides many a scientific and comprehensive solutions to rectify effects of incorrect directional placements in a horoscope, mismatch of planetary positions and improper alignment of *Vastu* elements. The five remedial measures indicated in the subsequent passages help in improving rhythm of a specific planet, and the particular direction under its domain.

8.3 Chanting of Mantra

Mantra serves as a focal point for various energy forms to establish a link between the human dimension and the cosmos. Mantra releases the mind from any hindrances and impediments at lower level of existence and elevates it to the *Akash-Tatwa* (ether).

In a *Japa*, the given *Mantra* is repeated thousands of times to produce cumulative energy stream.

A *Mantra* creates its own specific resonance in the Nada (subtle vibrations) domain. A deity or associated cosmic force can be evoked by chanting its unique *Mantra*. Any *Mantra* associated with a specific planet adds its vibrations to the lost portion of the aura to attain cosmic balance in human body and mind. Evil effects of a deficient direction of a *Vastu* are compensated by chanting of '*Mantra*' of the governing planet of that direction.

8.4 Application of Yantra

Yantra is basically a symbol. *Yantra* making process involves creating a rhythmic molecular memory on a metal piece through a ritual. Here, mystic codes of figures, numerals, symbols are engraved on a metal plate, and then the symbol is converted by rituals to project an aura. Many a times, enlightened persons give away gifts, which serve as carriers of their grace and cosmic bliss. These presents can also act as *Yantras* or cosmic carriers that help in aura rectification. By using primordial sounds (*Beej Mantras*), divine fire, smoke-vapours of divine plants, and harmonised water, the rituals create a quantum memory on metal pieces. These *Yantras* can be can be utilised in realising certain objectives in life. The use of specific *Yantras* in *Vastushastra* has been discussed in the next chapter.

8.5 Precious Stones, Pearls, and Jewels

Precious stones have wide-ranging effects on human aura, similar in nature to those originating from a *Yantra*. All gems have their own polarised energy spectrum representing specific planets through which cosmic envelope can be attained around the dweller and the dwelling. In case of precious stones, colour and light are additional elements apart from the quantum memory. It is customary to use these stones around certain points of human body, which are also classified by acupuncture theory as sensitive energy spots. Thus, the traditional practice of using gems can prove to be a comprehensive remedial measure at all levels. The following chart lists astrologically significant gems selected on the basis of planetary influence.

Planet	Primary Gem or Metal for Enhancing Planetary Virtues	Secondary / Alternate Precious Stone, Metal, or Herbal Roots
Sun रवि	Ruby माणिक	Copper ताम्र
Moon चंद्र	Pearls मोती	Silver रौप्य
Mars मंगल	Coral प्रवाल	Copper ताम्र
Mercury बुध	Emerald पांचू	Bronze पितल
Jupiter गुरु	Topaz पुष्कराज	Zinc जस्त
Venus शुक्र	Diamond वज्र	Silver रोप्य
Saturn शनि	Sapphire नीलमणी	Lead शिसम
Rahu राहु	Agate गोमेद	Lead शिसम
Ketu केतू	Azurite वैदुर्य	Lajawati Muli लाजावती मुली

Table 8.1: Precious Stones and Metals for Garnering Positive Planetary Energies

8.6 Colours

Frequency bands or vibrations of specific colours used in personal clothing and surroundings can compensate lost rhythms, and can effectively improve response of the external environment towards human entity. Light is one of the basic elements that improves and creates holistic environment. Directional deficiencies traced to colour flaws can be rectified by use of definite colours.

For selecting colours for a *Vastu*, Shri Ranga Chakra is an ideal guide. Even otherwise, zodiac sign of the owner and constellation projections can be applied in choosing colours suitable for *Vastu* decoration.

Zodiac Sign	Preferred Colour
Aries	Red
Taurus	White
Gemini	Green
Cancer	Pink
Leo	Off-white
Virgo	Whitish Green
Libra	White Cement
Scorpio	Red, Pink
Sagittarius	Golden Yellow
Capricorn	Brick Red
Aquarius	Blue, Pink
Pisces	Yellow, Bright White

Table 8.2: Choice of colours based on owner's zodiac sign

Direction	Planet	Colour
East	Sun	Bright White
Northeast	Jupiter	Golden Yellow
North	Mercury	Green
Northwest	Moon	White
West	Saturn	Blue
Southwest	Rahu	Green
South	Mars	Red, Pink
Southeast	Venus	Silver White

Table 8.3: Colour scheme based on directions and planets

In practice, people may opt for the first scheme when the *Vastu-Purush-Mandal* reflects positive aspects of the zodiac sign of the owner of a *Vastu* as per his natural horoscope. When horoscope details are not easily available, a *Vastu* analyst may suggest colour schemes based on the directional situation of a dwelling.

Zodiac	Element	Colour	Soul-mate	Friend	Adversary
Aries Leo Sagittarius	Fire	Red	Air Blue	Earth Yellow	Water White
Taurus Virgo Capricorn	Earth	Yellow	Water White	Fire Red	Air Blue
Gemini Libra Aquarius	Air	Blue	Fire Red	Water White	Earth Yellow
Cancer Scorpio Pisces	Water	White	Earth Yellow	Air Blue	Fire Red

Table 8.4: Shri Ranga Chakra (Zodiac Sign - Colour Schematic)

The affiliation of definite great elements with constellations and zodiac signs is utilised in Shri Raga Chakra for selection of directionwise colours. Any colour through its frequency spectrum can mimic specific great element and help in enhancing or subtracting directional virtues or flaws observed in a *Vastu*. A friendly colour accentuates the virtues of the great element, while a hostile colour diminishes the effects of the element.

8.7 Cosmic Baths

Bathing is of immense importance and almost a ritual in Eastern religions. Various types of oils, salts, and herbs are used as cleansing agents in a bath.

A person's bodily aura is a reflection of the cosmic aura, and skin being the most sensitive part of body, any change in bio-plasma due to bio-chemical processes initiated by oils, herbs, and salts has immediate effect on human aura. Skin cells are optically sensitive and show positive response to polarised light. Based on this fact ritualistic baths make use of divine waters, herbs, and divine light. In practice, various herbs and different metallic utensils are used according to the planetary effects. A person is blessed with cosmic virtues if he performs the cosmic bath ritual utilising proper herbs and vessels as determined by the planetary deficiencies in his natural horoscope.

Vastu-Dosha and Remedial Action

Planet	Plant / Herbs for Ritual Bath	Utensil / Vessel for Ritual Bath	Talisman for Wearing on Person
Sun रवि	Lajalu / Manjishtha लाजाळू / मंजिष्ठा	Copper ताम्र	बेलमूळ
Moon चंद्र	Koshtha कोष्ठ	Conch शंख	शिरणीमूळ
Mars मंगळ	Chikanamul चिकणमूळ	Silver रौप्य	नागजिव्हा
Mercury बुध	Gahula गेहुला	Earthen मृद्	वरदारा
Jupiter गुरु	Nagarmotha नागरमोठा	Gold कांचन	भारंगमूळ
Venus शुक्र	Safed Shiras सफेद शिरस	Silver रौप्य	वाघोटीमूळ
Saturn शनि	Halad हळद	Iron लोह	वाडूळ
Rahu राहु	Sharponkha शरपोंखा	Bull Horn शिंग	मलयचंदन
Ketu केतू	Lodha लोध्र	Sword Guard खड्गपात्र	अश्वगंधा

Table 8.5: Plants and herbs for use in ritualistic bath

There is another way of making the body sensitive for receiving planetary energies. At a auspicious time or *'Muhurta'* which matches with specific planetary influence, an individual may wear special herbs in the form of a talisman or a charm, on his person to ward off ill effects of malignant planetary conjunctions in natural and/or *Vastu* horoscope.

Cosmic ritual baths or use of talisman help in nullifying the evil influence of any Vastu-dosha on the persons residing in a *Vastu*.

In effect, many-sided approach is required in choosing remedial measures for improving a *Vastu* situation. As in *Vastu*-analysis, recourse to *Yogashastra*, Astrology, and Science proves helpful in arriving at a proper decision.

9. TANTRA, MANTRA, AND YOGA IN VASTU SCIENCE

In previous chapters we have seen how *Vastushastra* serves as a key for initiating a cycle of auspicious events in one's life. *Vastushastra* is an art of changing the fortunes of a person by understanding the impact of the *Jaivik* and *Pranik Urja* currents. In this chapter, we will first learn the *Tantra* (technique), then find *Mantra* remedies, and finally try to understand the *Yantra* applications.

9.1 Purva-Sanskara, Prarabdha, Jyotisha, and Vastukundli

Sanchita, *Prarabdha*, and *Kriyaman* form the trio of '*Karma*' principles in Eastern philosophy. In colloquial language it is best expressed in the proverb 'so shall thou beget the fruit as the seeds sowed'. In his birth a man brings along with him the accumulated results of his *Purva-Sanskara*. A horoscope is nothing but the mathematical representation of his deeds in the past life presented at the very time he is born. *Jyotisha* predicts the possibilities of improvement in personality factors or situation related to happiness or sorrow in his life, based on this very horoscope. *Vastushastra* in a sense gives remedial measures or provides solutions for the corresponding events associated with a personality. Changing the horoscope is beyond our scope, but it is always possible to alter a given *Vastu* situation so that natural energy flow is properly channelled through a Vastu to initiate the process of auspicious events. *Vastushastra* means establishing constructive link between *Swa* (self) and the *Kha* (ether/sky). Here, *Swa* implies *Purva-Sanskara* defined by relative planetary positions in astrology and *Kha* signifies the greatest element as per *Yogashastra* - the sky or the ether. Destiny and fate can render a man immobile, inactive, and dependent on others. *Darshanshastra* counters these very concepts. Its sub-branches establish a cycle of auspicious events and precedents, and in a way command the nature through mind, intellect, and talent.

Yogashastra aims at conversion of the *Manas* (mind) into *Gagan* (sky element) through the medium of *Pavan* (wind element). By controlling and channelling the breath and *Prana*, *Yogashastra* cleanses the effects of *Purva-Sanskara*. *Prana* is the creative link between the silent nature and the macroscopic world. *Vastushastra* is the discipline that controls and changes the universal form of this *Pranik* energy through manipulation of the four great elements - *Prithvi* (earth), *Aap* (water), *Tej* (fire) and *Vayu* (wind).

The divinities assigned to the *Vastu-Purush-Mandal* are based on the effect of these four great elements on the sub-directions (Northeast, Northwest, Southeast, and Southwest) in the *Mandal*. The element water is associated with the Northeast direction, fire with the Southeast, earth with the Southwest, and wind with the Northwest direction. The disciplined and balanced form of an occupied *Vastu* largely depends on the due importance given to these four great elements, or in effect to the four sub-directions. Similarly, in a natural horoscope, a group of two zodiac signs are bunched around each of the sub-directions, while the main four directions are influenced by the zodiac signs *Mesha* (Aries), *Karka* (Cancer), *Tula* (Libra), and *Makar* (Capricorn). At the dawn when the solar cycle becomes active, the characteristics of the sub-directions are also in charged state - element water in the Northeast, element fire in the Southeast, element earth in the Southwest, and element wind in the Northwest direction. It is the very reason why the *Brahma-Muhurta* or the early morning time is considered an auspicious time. This is the period when natural forces are in complete balance and harmony with each other. *Vastushastra* all the time strives to catch hold of the benefits of this *Ish-Kal* or *Akshay-Kal* or *Brahma-Ghati* through its well-designed principles. It can be said that Vastushastra is the technique of creating in the macroscopic world, the currents of auspicious *Chandra-Nadi* present in the invisible nature.

By establishing the *Prithvi Tatva* in the Southwest direction, the natural *Jaivik* and *Pranik* flows receive boost from the

Northeast direction due to the enhanced gravitation in the Southwest and thus, allowing the *Jaivik* and *Pranik* energies to join into a harmonic merger called Priti Sangam. *Akash Tatva* is the source for all events and these events flow along the natural energy currents. The *Prithvi Tatva* of the Southwest, the *Jal-Tatva* of the Northeast, the *Agni Tatva* of the Southeast, and the *Vayu Tatva* of the Northwest in a balanced state provide the *Vastu* with cosmic auspicious event-horizon.

9.2 Laws of Nature and Vastu Rules

Rishi Kannada has described the process of transformation of *Akash Tatva* into *Vayu Tatva*, *Vayu Tatva* into *Agni Tatva*, *Agni Tatva* into *Jal Tatva* and then creation of atoms of the *Prithvi Tatva* from the *Jal Tatva*. The atoms having *Panch-Maha-Bhuta* characteristics are created through catalytic action of the *Panch-Matras* - *Shabda* (word), *Sparsh* (touch), *Roop* (form), *Rasa* (taste), and *Gandha* (flavour). By God's grace, the energetic macro world has been generated from the eight-fold secret nature. Human intelligence is a reflection of the divine touch, and its influence permeates through all the sciences. It detours from the scientific premise to scientific principle to metaphysics to semi-divine perspective to spirituality.

Astrology describes the qualitative development of the eight directions, twelve zodiac signs, and twenty-seven constellations in terms of the *Panch-Maha-Bhuta* characteristics. *Vastushastra* describes the *Panch-Maha-Bhutas* based attainment of divine characteristics by the eight directions. *Yogashastra* describes the control exercised by the *Ida* (Chandra Nadi), *Pingala* (Surya Nadi), and *Shushubhna* (Brahma Nadi) on the eight directions. The classification in all these three disciplines is mediated through the four parameters - vibrations, waves, sound, and light. To design a perfect Vastu, it is essential that the foundations of these disciplines be studied in detail.

The benevolent trees, benevolent metals, benevolent directions, benevolent planets as detailed in astrology can be used as remedial measures against directional flaws (*Disha-dosha*) encountered in *Vastushastra*. Every direction can be provided with the necessary gravitation or levitation to propel the natural energy flows. Additionally, parameters like colour, taste, and form based on the *Yogashastra* terminology of *Panch-Maha-Bhutas* can be utilised for removing the effects of *Vastu-dosha*.

9.3 Tantra

All the impediments obstructing the smooth natural energy flow can be removed by employing *Vastushastra* techniques. A study and insight into the natural energy forms can provide us with tools to set aside every type of barrier.

By utilising the *Jaivik* and *Pranik* energy flows as controlled by cosmic energy cycle, *Vastushastra* defines the techniques to enhance the life-sustaining qualities of a *Vastu*. *Vastushastra* derives its strength from various disciplines - *Yogashastra*, Astrology, *Ayurved*, Music, and Physical Sciences.

A *Mantra* garners cosmic and bodily forces and concentrates these through a ritual. A *Yantra* is a focal point of the visible and the knowable, and gathers visually *manifest* energies. *Tantra* makes use of the fact that *Mantra* and *Yantra* can act in cohesion and can complement each other.

9.3.1 Planets and Earthly Symbols

Astrology considers that the directions Southeast, South, and West are directions of strength for the planets Venus, Mars, and Saturn respectively. Hence, स्फटिक (sphatik) or a crystal representing Venus is placed in the Southeast direction, copper symbolising Mars is assigned to the Southern zone, and iron or lead identified with Saturn is utilised in the West zone. From scientific perspective, it can be noticed that the metal copper serves as a purifying agent and is an excellent conductor of heat and electricity, enabling it to control and guide the micro-electric currents encountered in the South zone. Importance of placing copper in the South can be understood in terms of characteristics of *Pranik* and *Jaivik Urja* currents. Since the *Pranik* energy current transits over an area from the East to the West via the South, copper, a conductor of Pranik currents should be placed at the transition point, i.e., the South. Copper also enables the North to South *Jaivik Urja* current to move in the Westerly direction. Thus, copper can influence the flow characteristics of the *Pranik* and *Jaivik Urja*, forcing these currents to flow in unison from the South to the West, simulating the Northeast type qualities of the *Vastu-Purush-Mandal* in the Southwest zone itself.

9.3.2 Bells

Resonating sound is the characteristic and quality of a bell. Sound emanating from a specific shape is endowed with virtuous properties. When this virtue serves as a linking bridge between the inner and outer spaces, the sound is called the primordial sound. In Eastern philosophy primordial sounds are perceived as links between an individual and the humanity. In Chinese Feng-Shui discipline, this type of sound is considered as a cleansing medium. In Christian traditions, bells are associated with Churches and Divinity. In Buddhist culture, bells are used as a catalyst to transcend the mind.

Bells generally have a pyramidal shape. These are cast from an amalgam of five metals. The resonating sound of a bell has characteristic rhythm and harmony. It creates divine order by imitating the primordial sound *AUM* and reverberating it in a repetitive manner, as if in a Japa. Meditation bells which when rubbed with a wooden stick produce vibrations equivalent to the vibrations of root *Mantra - AUM -* are quite common in Tibetan Lama Dynasties.

As described in scriptures and ancient texts,

A of AUM gives *Jagruti*

U of AUM gives *Swapna*, and

M of AUM gives *Sushupti*

Reverberations in chanting *AUM* represent *Turiya* state. Bells resonate and echo these reverberations for a prolonged time in an extended space. *Turiya* is the fourth state of consciousness representing creativity and completeness. Resounding bells bless the environment with virtues of this *Turiya* state.

To remove Vastu-dosha of any direction, bells are the simplest media. Bells used in combination with crystals become a very effective tool in *Vastu* science. The reverberations of bells have

Tantra, Mantra, and Yoga in Vastu Science 81

profound natural quality to improve vibrations and waves of a space. According to the eastern tradition of spiritual practices, these reverberations transform the voids in space, which are essentially the wombs of creation.

9.3.3 Crystals and Mantra Archana

As a purifier and symbol of auspicious events, Sphatik or a crystal has its own importance in Chinese Feng-Shui technique. A स्फटिकमाला or a chain of crystals is used in routine जाप (Jap) or meditative chanting and other religious rituals. The *Shiva*, *Shaligram*, and *Lingam* in Hindu religion symbolise Goddess forms. In fact, these forms are crystals provided with definite forms. According to the Feng-Shui concepts, a crystal is a link between the microcosm and the macrocosm. It enables the cosmic energy to grace the human mindset.

The Hindu spiritual rites of the *Mantra Archana* (offering of *Mantra*) and *Panchamrut Abhishek* (sprinkling of hombre of five liquids) are said to initiate focusing of human aspirations on the crystalline *Shivlinga*. Here, a crystal is used as a solid catalyst for creating invigorating energy space for human psyche and in precipitating the confluence of *Pranik* and *Jaivik* energies. In the Shiva Temples and Pyramids, the outer boundaries touch the macrocosm or the divine space. The inner confines of these structures allow for the constructive merger of the cosmic energy and the *Mantra*-stimulated *Jaivik* energy at the crystal, which represents the energy of human yearnings and desires. In a broader perspective, the *Chid-akash* (inner space) and *Vaishvik-akash* (cosmic space) are unified into one body.

The crystal has its own importance for the Southeast direction. In the Southeast zone, the crystal acts as an impeller of energy flow, enabling the *Pranik* energy flow to establish its bearings in the cosmic energy cycle and receive the necessary recharging.

9.3.4 Use of Metals against Disha-dosha

In astrology, the Western direction is the direction of strength for the planet Saturn. Saturn is considered to be a negative influence on divine qualities, and a sink and terminator of every possible energy form. Even the source of *Pranik* energy, the Sun, sets in the West only. Modern experimental nuclear physics indicates that maximum cosmic radiation is received from the West direction. According to *Avak-Hada Chakra*, the metal lead represents Saturn. In nuclear technology lead is used in atomic reactors, X-ray aprons, and nuclear shields for its excellent radiation absorption qualities. Now we can broadly correlate the ancient logic behind symbolically using lead in the West direction, which is ruled by Saturn, and the modern concepts of protection against excessive radiation reaching the West zone.

The West direction is considered to be on amicable terms with all termination processes. By placing a lead-chain in the West, the direction achieves completeness from Vastushastra point of view. The *Pranik* and *Jaivik* energy currents complete the natural energy cycle when lead-rings are placed in the West and the copper plates in the South. Copper provides the necessary conductive medium for movement and flow for the energy currents, pushing these towards the sink of lead in the West direction. By guiding the energy cycles associated with a *Vastu* into their own natural directional paths, a type of Lunar flow (*Chandra Pravah*) gets attached to the *Vastu*, and endows the Vastu with superior virtues like divine-shield and cosmic envelope.

Now that we are conversant with the *Tantra* or technique of achieving natural directional flows for the *Pranik* and *Jaivik* energies as per *Vastushastra* principles, we can take a look at the *Mantra* concepts.

9.4 Mantra

The letter त्र in मंत्र symbolises a protective shield. मंत्र is defined as the technique for providing the mind or the Mana with an envelope of protection. The human existence is directly identified with the concept of mind. By protecting the mind, *Mantra* in fact helps in preservation of the human existence. By following the laws of natural energy cycles, human existence automatically imbibes the techniques of self-preservation.

In previous chapters we have noted that the nature is constituted by *Panch-Maha-Bhutas*. Its characteristics and

Tantra, Mantra, and Yoga in Vastu Science

qualities are influenced by the *Tanmatras* having virtues of the *Panch-Maha-Bhutas*. The *Shabda* (words) having Tanmatra form is an amalgamation of *Sparsh* (touch), *Roop* (shape), *Rasa* (nature), and *Gandha* (smell). Using mind as the medium, Mantra has the powers to lift the mind from the worldly level to the cosmic level. *Mantras* have the microscopic form of nature as constituted by *Panch-Maha-Bhutas*. Further, *Mantras* reflect the oneness and unity of the nature. Therefore *Mantras* have wide ranging effect on both the *Prakriti* and the *Srushti*. Through *Mantra*, one can surrender the mind to the divine scheme of the *Purush*, the *Chaitanya, Ishwar-tatva* (the divine element).

Vastu-tantra induces in external environment an omniscient centre of power that can bring about positive changes in the inner persona. Here, the route for an individual's journey towards success is from the outer environs to the inner confines of mind. On the other hand, *Mantra-Shakti* makes the mind a centre of power, and the cosmic energy travels from within the body to the space outside. As per *Mantrashastra*, the entire atmosphere and the space is filled with primordial sounds, the *Akshar Varnamala* (the basic alphabet). *Mantrashastra* in fact, commands the flow of Pran Shakti throughout the atmosphere. Akshar *Varnamala* letters can be classified according to the specific element of *Panch-Maha-Bhutas* these represent.

क ख ग घ ङ	पृथ्वी
त थ द ध न	वायु
प फ ब भ म	आकाश
ट ठ ड ढ ण	अग्नि
च छ ज झ ञ	जल
य र ल व श ष स ह क्ष ज्ञ	संकल्प सिद्धी
अ आ इ ई उ ऊ	विद्युत चुंबकीय
अ:	स्वरभाव

Chart 9.1: Akshar Varnamala & Panch-Maha-Bhutas

Sound modulated through *Uccharan Shastra* (technique of pronunciation) and *Mantrashastra* imparts specific rhythm to the atmospheric atoms. The rhythmic impulse charges the creative energy of the entire space, which in turn influences the nature to facilitate execution of certain tasks.

Mantrashastra has in itself the capacity to impart qualities of the microscopic universe to the macroscopic attributes of nature. *Pran Shakti* or creative energies that are circulated through an object charged with *Mantrashastra*, prove helpful to human beings. *Havan* (fire sacrifice) of certain plants, modulated and controlled *Mantragaan* (recitation of Mantras), and excitation of universal *Beej Mantras* through rhythmic notes of certain musical instruments in a way connect the mind and body with the *Akash Tatva* and induce flow of *Pran Shakti* through the human dimension. Recitation of *Mantras* proves fruitful in improving the virtuous qualities of a *Vastu*.

Insight of astrology is helpful in neutralising planetary ill effects, and directional flaws can be corrected with the aid of *Vastushastra*. *Mantrashastra* regime in itself can take care of both these factors. Indeed, the medium of sound can bestow divine grace to a *Vastu* in a most natural and normal manner.

9.5 Vastu Yantra

Vastu Yantra concepts pertain to three different aspects - divine element, worldly element, and spiritual element. Here, we discuss several items of *Vastu Yantra*. For specific directions, *Vastu Yantra* utilises particular items associated with a planet as per the direction-wise classification of the planets in astrology. The inspiration for this exercise is drawn from the *Avak-Hada Chakra*. Passage of light can be influenced by the use of mirrors. A crystal (स्फटीक, Sphatik) is known for its prowess in wish-fulfilment and attaining success in Chinese Feng-Shui technique. Polarisation of light by water surface, a concept from modern science, has been successfully used in *Vastu Yantra*. Using the *Vastu Yantras*, one can rectify various *Vastu-Doshas* or distorted rhythms of a direction. Chinese Feng-Shui acknowledges importance of musical items like jingle bells, which can produce natural sounds and rhythms. Trees and plants, beneficial for ecology and environment, can also be used in correcting *Vastu-dosha*. *Avak-Hada Chakra* (अवकहडा चक्र) best describes the correlation between the trees, star constellations, and *Panch-Maha-Bhutas*. The benevolent trees (*Aradhya Vriksha*) associated with divine constellations (*Dev Nakshatra*), as detailed in *Avak-Hada Chakra* prove useful in attaining environmental equilibrium. Christmas tree is best suited for rectifying certain disturbed rhythms, because of its pyramidal shape. Pyramid is the best known controller for guiding cosmic energy, and the shape itself adds aesthetic beauty to a *Vastu*. Stones like marble that can polarise light and cosmic energy, could be utilised in specific directions for flooring etc.

Eight types of *Vastu Yantras* have been discussed in detail, in the following passages.

Ishanya Patra ईशान्य पात्र

Vayavya Sanvadini वायव्य संवादिनी

Pyramid पिरॅमिड

Urdhwa Gurutwa उर्ध्व गुरुत्व

Nairutya Pushkarini नैऋत्य पुष्करिणी

Agneya Sanskarini आग्नेय संस्करिणी

Dakshin Tamra Samvahak दक्षिण ताम्र संवाहक

Sphatik Sahasamvedak स्फटीक सहसंवेदक

9.5.1 ईशान्य पात्र (Ishanya Patra)

The Northeast is the most important direction in *Vastushastra*. It is the source of all the cosmic energies. The Northeast lies at the central zone in the paths of *Pranik* and *Jaivik* energy flows. Relatively ideal geomagnetically balanced zone is observed in the Northeast only. This direction is deprived of the qualities associated with source points of energy, if Northeast openings are blocked in the *Vastu*, or if toilets or staircase are located in this zone. Ishanya Patra (vessel for the Northeast) simulates the energy source characteristics, if placed in the Northeast zone. Light is reflected by the mirror of the ईशान्य पात्र, induces parallel constructive flow the Pranik and Jaivik energies. The *Shri Chakra* embossed on the mirror is an ancient Indian mystic symbol that creates a fresh stream of cosmic energy flow. The copper in this Yantra is a known purifying agent. In astrology, copper is a symbol of Mars on the earth, and has its own advantages. The metal silver is associated with Moon. The Moon as well as the Northeast zone has qualities of Jal Tatva, the basic element water. *Sphatik* or a crystal helps in giving fruition to human endeavours. It polarises and harnesses cosmic energy. *Sphatik* is the embodiment of the celestial being. Infinite polarised waves of light are circulated in the atmosphere due to the crystal placed in an *Abhishek Patra* is sprinkled with a continuous stream of water. The water in the copper vessel polarises light in an even plane, imparting a creative form of cosmic energy to the surrounding space. Chinese Feng-Shui discipline considers the mirror, the crystal, and the water to be universal purifiers. The *Shiva Yantra* designed by Shri Adi Shankaracharya is also placed in the copper vessel. Astrology considers that the crystal, the silver, and the water symbolise the Moon. Since all these three items are located in the Northeast zone, the auspicious *Ida-Chandra Nadi* current starts flowing through the *Vastu*, providing it with a divine grace.

Plate 1: Ishanya Yantra

The *Ishanya Yantra* is in a sense *Sapta Guna Vardhini* (harbinger of seven virtues) as the copper purifies, silver induces Chandra

Tantra, Mantra, and Yoga in Vastu Science

Nadi flow, water polarises, crystal provides divine grace, mirror enhances the source charateristics of the Northeast zone and the *Shri Yantra* and *Shiva Yantra* establishe the cosmic power centre in the *Vastu*.

9.5.2 वायव्य संवादिनी (Vayavya Sanvadini)

In *Vastu-Purush-Mandal*, *Pavan* is the Goddess of the Northwest direction. The *Vayu Tatva*, symbolic of vacillation, movement, sound energy and power imparts these qualities to the *Vastu* from the Northwest direction. This direction is endowed with qualities for inducing the flow of cosmic energy in the *Vastu*.

As per the *Vastu-Purush-Mandal*, Goddesses like *Pavan*, *Som*, *Ish*, and *Aditya* who symbolise rejuvenation and growth govern the zone right from the Northwest to the East. For the family residing in the *Vastu*, interaction and rapport with one another is influenced by this direction only. Lord Hanuman is one of the most important members of *Sapta Chiranjiva* or the seven divine sons. Hanuman is also known as *Pavan Putra* (son of the Goddess Pavan). *Pavan* takes the form of *Pran* in the human body. Yogashastra gives immense importance to the trinity - *Mana* (mind), *Pavan* (wind), and *Gagan* (sky or ether). *Pavan* helps in enjoining the immeasurable energy of the *Gagan* with the *Mana*. The *Goddess Pavan* handles the important task of creative circulation of the cosmic energy and the *Pran Shakti* in the *Vastu* from the Northwest direction. *Vayu Tatva* is associated with the colour 'blue' in Yogashastra. Creative use of blue colour can activate the *Vayu Tatva* in the *Vastu*. The वायव्य संवादिनी utilises a blue-coloured '*Mala*', blue crystal, and *jingle* bells made of '*Panch Dhatu*' (an amalgam of five metals) to bestow on the *Vastu* divine bliss and to promote better understanding and interaction between the people residing therein. Feng-Shui stresses the use of jingle bells to remove negative energies from the Vastu. In Lama rituals and in Buddhist culture in general, the cyclic revolutions of some special kind of bells are considered important for linking the *Mana* with *Gagan*. As we have been repeatedly pointing out that a crystal encloses within itself the power centre that influences human aspirations, plans, and endeavours. As such, placing a blue crystal in the Northwest direction provides a shield against indecision or inaction.

9.5.3 पिरॅमिड (Pyramid)

The word *pyramid* is interpreted as 'pyre at mid' i.e. fire in the middle zone. Pyramidal structure is associated with many mysterious constants in geometry, 'Golden Ratio', and the natural growth shape, the 'Helix'. The geometrical constant π (3.14) and the golden ratio factor 1.618 play a major role in the construction of a pyramid.

The world over, Egypt is known for its *pyramids*. But the formation of pyramidal structures in Hindu temples is more sophisticated and qualitatively superior in their natural shapes. Egyptian pyramids were built for preventing decomposition of dead bodies of the Pharaohs through accentuation of *Prithvi Tatva* qualities. But the pyramidal structures found in Hindu temples reflect the rejuvenating forms of the *Panch-Maha-Bhutas*.

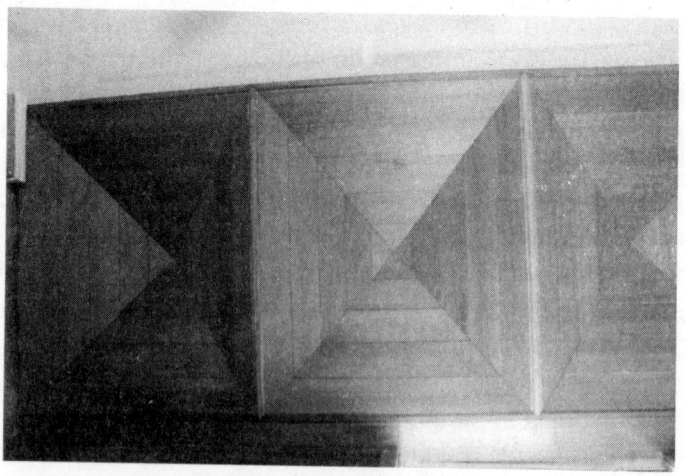

Plate 2: Pyramids

In Hindu *pyramids* the essential virtues of the *Akash Tatva* pervade the structure in a most natural way. The outer pyramidal shape and the inner round dome shaped structure ensure that pyramid serves as a bridge to simulate qualities of the vast cosmic *Akash Tatva* in

Tantra, Mantra, and Yoga in Vastu Science

one-third area of the internal dome shaped '*Chid Akash*' interacting with the human beings at a personal level.

By meditating in such a charged space, a devotee's personal aspirations and endeavours derive the necessary boost in energy. The traditional practice in South India of constructing pyramidal divine '*Gopurs*' in front of or in four corners outside a temple serves the same purpose. The '*Gopurs*' and the '*Shikhars*' of a temple are built in such a way that vast cosmic energy finds its natural form inside a temple and energy envelope is created around the worshippers. The Buddhist and Feng-Shui practice of providing roofs having pyramid-like shapes follow the same logic. These pyramidal structures create the necessary ambience for unification of the body with the *Akash Tatva*, the mind with the *Pavan* and the soul with the *Gagan* on the path to divine evolution.

Square base is a speciality of Egyptian pyramids. *Yogashastra* endows a square shape with qualities of the *Prithvi Tatva*. We can infer that Egyptian pyramid builders had given special attention to the *Prithvi Tatva*. But, the Indian pyramidal domes give due importance to the shapes like square, triangle, circle etc. We can conclude that the Indian pyramids like domes are the best sources for divine and creative energy space.

चतुरस्रं चार्धचंद्रं त्रिकोणं वर्तुळिं स्मृतम्
बिन्दुभिस्तु नभो ज्ञेयमाकारैस्तत्व लक्षणम्

(Square, semi-lunar triangle, circle, and then specific points are the sequence of shapes that generates *Prithvi*, *Aap*, *Tej*, *Vayu* and *Akash Tatva* in that order - *Shiv Swarodaya Shastra*)

The pyramidal shape can nullify all forms of negative energy, and is an excellent remedy on various *Vastu-doshas*.

9.5.4 ऊर्ध्व गुरुत्व (Urdhwa Gurutwa)

The Prithvi-Tatva manifests from the Southwest direction. The massiveness, gravitational pull, and stability associated with the *Prithvi-Tatva* enhance the qualities of the Southwest direction. During daytime the Southwest zone is exposed to intense solar radiation for almost eight hours at a stretch, leading to high temperatures. The natural geomagnetic fluxlines in this zone face obstructions and are disturbed due to excessive heat. To enhance the *Prithvi-Tatva*, it is possible to simulate massiveness in the Southwest zone through उर्ध्व गुरुत्व (*Urdhwa Gurutwa*, enhanced gravity) technique.

Plate 3: Urdhwa Gurutwa Yantra

The two factors considered in devising remedial measures for Southwest zone are; (I) the colour yellow is identified with *Prithvi-Tatva*, and (II) *pyramids* have the capacity to annihilate negative energy currents. The *Urdhwa Gurutwa* concepts indicate that placing of a solid stone in the Southwest direction, or fixing such a stone on the Southwest wall, or location of heavy furniture in this zone can lead to enhancement of the *Prithvi-Tatva*. Equally effective measures are, placing of *pyramids* and using yellow colour in this zone.

9.5.5 नैऋत्य पुष्करिणी (Nairutya Pushkarini)

In a plot or *Vastu-kshetra*, gravitational mass can be simulated and stability achieved through नैऋत्य पुष्करिणी (*Nairutya Pushkarini*, Southwest pond).

Plate 4: Nairutya Pushkarini

The *Prithvi-Tatva* and the *Jal-Tatva* are considered to be on friendly terms. Location of water in the Southwest zone can help in improving the qualities of that zone. In the Southwest zone, solid stone masonry should be arranged one meter thick above the ground level, and an artificial pond should be constructed on this platform. The *Prithvi-Tatva* can be enhanced with the yellow decorative stone used for this pond. In the Feng-Shui technique, a lotus is treated as an auspicious and divine object. The circular shaped leaves of a lotus are considered to be divine and are used as a medium for the removal of negative energies. A tortoise, symbol of stability and wealth, can also be placed in such a pond. The Hindu religion considers a tortoise to be a carrier of celestial energies. The flowing water, the divine yellow lotus, the circular lotus leaves recommended by Feng-Shui, the manifestation of *Prithvi-Tatva* through yellow stones, and the dynamic stability through a live tortoise make the नैरुत्य पुष्करिणी a unique *Yantra* for enhancing the virtuous qualities of the Southwest direction.

9.5.6 अग्नेय संस्करिणी (Agneya Sanskarini)

The natural cycle of *Pranik Urja* commences from the East direction. The *Aditya* form of the Sun is associated with the East direction. As the name suggests, अग्नेय (*Agneya*, अग्नि = fire) or the Southeast direction faces the fiery form of the Sun. The atmosphere in the vicinity of the Southeast face of the *Vastu* gets heated up due to solar radiation. As a symbolic reflection of external warm conditions, an *Uccha-Ushna Jyoti* or an intense flame is lit up in the Southeast zone inside the Vastu. In essence, the fire in the Southeast direction gives the necessary impetus to the *Pranik Urja* cycle originating from the East direction.

As per astrology, the planet Venus influences the Southeast direction. Therefore, a crystal, which can polarise energies, should be used in the Southeast direction. Due to the crystal in this direction, the *Pranik Urja* cycle receives the necessary acceleration through the polarised solar energy. The *Jaivik Urja* from the North direction and the *Pranik Urja* coming from the East direction receive energetic impulse from the crystal or the *Uccha-Ushna* Jyoti.

9.5.7 दक्षिण ताम्र संवाहक (Dakshin Tamra Samvahak)

The high solar temperatures in the South direction lead to chaotic conditions in the geomagnetic fluxlines. The *Jaivik Urja* flowing from the North direction to the South loses its unidirectional properties due to the rising temperature gradient in the South zone. Radiation particles can get trapped in the distorted magnetic fluxlines - a potentially harmful environment for human beings. The South direction is also known as the direction of *Yama* or the direction of death. An opening in the South zone leads to a mutual opposing interaction of currents of *Jaivik Urja* and the *Pranik Urja*. *Jiva* (living being) versus *Pran* (life force) implies death - a symbolism associated with goddess *Yama* in the South direction as per *Vastu-Purush-Mandal*. Copper serves as the ideal conductor for diversion of inconsistent *Jaivik* and *Pranik* energy flows. It balances the hostile currents of the *Jaivik* and *Pranik* energies.

The planet Mars rules the South direction as per astrology. On this Earth, copper is symbolic of Mars. The ancient logic of establishing the link between the South direction, the planet Mars, and copper is indeed amazing. This ancient technique of arriving at universal truth through proper observations is reflected in the saying ज्ञानात् ध्यानम् विशिष्यते (Meditation proves more beneficial than a priori knowledge - *Bhagwad Gita*).

The *Jaivik Urja* from the North direction and the *Pranik Urja* from the East direction merge into a unidirectional current through

Tantra, Mantra, and Yoga in Vastu Science

the use of copper. The universal energy cycle can be implemented in the small *Vastu*-space itself through the conducting metal, copper.

Bhoumya Yantra (mystic symbols embossed on a hexagonal copper plate) is a powerful remedy on *Vastu-dosha* associated with the South direction. It is generally used in combination with *Dakshin Tamra Samvahak* (conducting copper plates in the South zone) as an antidote on *Vastu* pollution due to South side *Vastu-dosha*.

Plate 5: Dakshin Tamra Samvahak and Bhoumya Yantra

9.5.8 स्फटीक सहसंवेदक (Sphatik Sahasamvedak)

A *Sphatik* or a crystal establishes a link between the microcosm and the macrocosm. In a sense, a crystal operates a feedback mechanism in which the dreams and aspirations of human beings that constitute the microcosm are received by crystal and then transmitted in a modulated form to the cosmos or the macrocosm. These desires are processed by the macro *Akash-Tatva* and redirected to human aspirants through the medium of the crystal, with necessary energy recharging.

The crystal reinforces the will power of a human being, so that he can carry out his plans without any hindrance. The ancient Hindu sciences and the Chinese Feng-Shui technique acknowledge the crystal as a source of divine power. Depending on the *Vastu-dosha* encountered, a crystal can be worn by a person, or can be located in a specific direction all by itself or as a part of a *Vastu-Yantra*.

The *Vastu-Yantras* discussed above can be used either separately or as a combination, depending on *Vastu-dosha* encountered and the actual potentiality of various directions for enhancing virtues.

9.6 Practical Vastu Remedies
9.6.1 Use of Mirrors
Sometimes the North and East sides of a room or a house are completely blocked by wall construction. This type of *Vastu-dosha* can be countered by the use of mirrors.

Plate 6: Mirrors for enhancing positive energy streams

The North and East are source directions for *Jaivik Urja* and *Pranik Urja* respectively. Blockage of these streams by the walls can be removed by using mirrors on these directions to initiate and provide channel for smooth flow of positive energies. Mirror on

Tantra, Mantra, and Yoga in Vastu Science

the North wall simulates large North-South length, a virtuous quality in *Vastushastra*. In the plate shown, notice the large sized mirrors on the North and East walls. Apart from this, a lunar shaped water surface has been provided in the Northeast corner to promote a cycle of auspicious events.

9.6.2 Water Body in Northeast Zone

Lunar shaped exposed water source placed in the Northeast zone is considered auspicious in *Vastushastra*. It enhances the polarised positive energy flow in the surroundings and blesses the household or premises with grace and wealth.

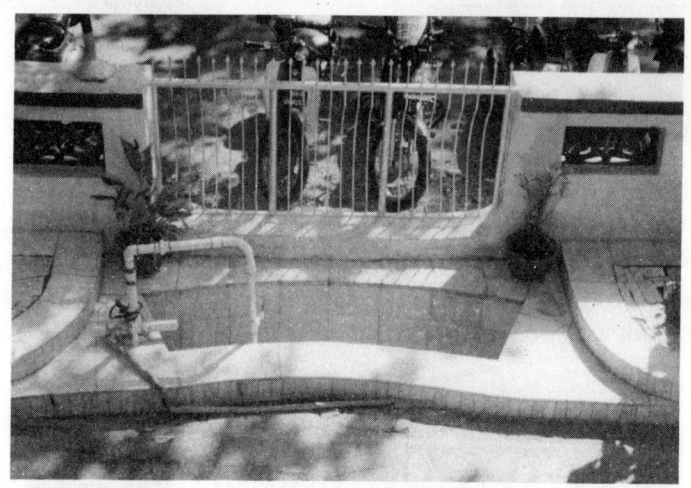

Plate 7: Lunar shaped water surface in Northeast direction

As shown in the plate, a curved (lunar shaped) water pond has been constructed in marble cladding in the Northeast zone. Additionally, opening in the compound wall adds to virtuous qualities of this zone.

9.6.3 Pyramidal Roofs and Ceilings

Pyramids are extensively used in *Vastushastra* to counter the *Vastu-dosha* in Southwest, West, and South zones.

Plate 8: Wooden pyramidal ceiling in extended Southwest

In Plate 8, wooden pyramidal ceiling has been provided inside an office room in the extended Southwest zone. Additionally, part portion of Southwest side window has suitably closed in conformity with Vastu tenets. Generally, for households, pyramids are not used inside a bedroom.

Plate 9: Use of pyramids outside Southern entrance

Pyramids can be used for blocking negative energy streams from the South side. In Plate 9 notice that black glass panels have suitably covered windows and door openings on South. Multiple pyramids have been placed to restrict negative streams.

9.6.4 Glass Bricks
The transparent glass bricks allow for natural light inside a room during daytime.

Plate 10: Glass bricks

In a case where the East, Northeast directions are blocked due to wall constructions and windows have not been provided, glass bricks can be used in place of regular bricks for part portion of the wall for initiating flow of *Pranik Urja* and *Jaivik Urja* from the source directions East, and North respectively.

9.6.5 Loading of Southwest
We have earlier seen use of *Urdhwa Gurutwa Yantra* for *Vastu-dosha* in Southwest zone. But this use is restricted to confines of a house. For larger areas, ill effects due to Southwest *Disha-dosha* can be controlled to a large extend by loading the Southwest side.

Plate 11: Heavy stone pillar in Southwest corner

As shown in Plate 11, Southwest loading can be achieved by construction of a heavy stone pillar in the corner with height in excess of average compound wall. This construction is in tune with the helix concept of *Vastushastra*.

All the *Vastu Yantras* and *Vastu* remedies have to be used with due consideration to relative effects of various *Vastu-dosha*.

10. ENERGY CONCEPT IN TEMPLE ARCHITECTURE

Eastern philosophy is based on the concept of five great elements, with the living being symbolically representing the energetic form of these elements. The same logic is discernible in the *Panch-Kosha* (five vessels) concept from the *Upanishads*. All rituals and religious activities are directed towards - (I) transformation of lower energetic vessel into a higher vessel, and (II) attaining the ultimate correlation between the most subtle element and existence.

Temple architecture in India represents this concept of evolution and radical changes. The complex energy forms and finer elements are intertwined with deities, trees, plants, colours, shapes and forms in the temple architecture. Different deities in the temple represent body, mind, intellect and the sub-components. These deities are then linked to the cosmos by associating them with specific directions. This philosophy establishes a chain of relationships between micro level elements and the macro level existence. The *Mandalas* (rings) available in temples are essentially charts of existence, transformations, and energetics.

The purpose of all rituals is directed towards reshaping of human psyche, transformation of individual perception into global perception, and radical changes in personal thoughts, desires, and ambitions. The space or sky is reshaped in temple architecture through domes, pyramids, various shapes and forms to provide maximum rhythmic response to achieve the desired results.

The characteristics and energies of the five great elements indicate that the finer the element in order of existence, the powerful is its control over the low-level existence. Earth, water, wind, fire, and ether have increasing degree of fineness as also higher energy content. Sky or ether is represented by spaces and has control over the other four elements. Correlating inner spaces with outer spaces is the essence of *Vastushastra*. The moment a right relationship is established between inner and outer being, cosmic bliss starts showering on the individual. This is what is termed as a change in the *Prarabdha* or the change in the destiny of the human being.

All religious rituals have a definite aim - transformation of the lower energy formats in the human being into the energy form of the outer spaces, or the sky, or the global being that is immensity. A suitable medium is provided by the sky as shaped by the domes and *pyramids*. A deity in the temple is a medium to absorb all the individual desires suitably transformed by rituals. The '*Deep-Mala*' (vertical fire pillar) in the line of the deity's vision in the outer space of the temple serves as the bridge linking the inner vessel of collective desires represented by the deity with outer space or sky that is global immensity. This fire pillar has a characteristic shape, which points towards the sky. A divine fire, which is the purifying factor in the temples, is lit using *ghee* (butter-oil) made from cow's milk. Through this fire circulates a rhythmic ascending energy form. Deity's vision is normally aligned to the North or the East directions, which are the sources of Jaivik Urja or positive energies.

The basic philosophy and foundations of temple architecture are reflected in details such as;

* polarisation of sunlight by the water-body in the Northeast,
* reshaping the desires of the devotee through rhythmic geometric format of sky element,
* creation of '*Naad-Sankash*' (sound space) with harmonic vibrations of primordial sounds, '*Mantras*', and ringing of bells,
* controlling the energy dynamics through the deity as the catalyst agent, and
* linking the inner space of desires and prayers to outer spaces through the '*Deep Mala*'.

The theme of Eastern philosophy rests on '*Mana*', '*Pavan*', and '*Gagan*' (mind, wind, and sky). Wind is the bridge for the mind to ascend to the sky. The holistic concept of evolution is defined in terms of the medium - the wind. Wind represents both, the sound and the sky. Therefore, primordial sounds are the keys to reinforcing the bond between the mind and the sky. Controlling the wind element at individual level is called '*Pranayam*'. We can say that the temple architecture provides a natural stage of '*Pranayam*', not with any definite individual efforts, but through various forms, shapes, rituals, and sounds. These parameters establish a unique path for correlating the wind and the sky. Domes and pyramids in the temple transform the sound to a '*Mandala*' (spherical response). The echo of this rhythmic primordial sound takes the wind to the sky. The '*Gurutatva*' (the master element) is described as '*Akhand Mandalakaram*'. This implies that the rhythmic '*Mandala*' created by the echo of primordial sounds activates the '*Gurutatva*' in the human mind.

To summarise, temple architecture in the Eastern thought creates a space for holistic atmosphere of natural *Pranayam* suitable for any individual. Echo of primordial sounds enters the limitless finer circles beyond the audible range and helps the mind to ascend from '*Saguna*' state (existence having a form) to '*Nirguna*' state (formless existence). The tradition of '*Aarati*', i.e., chorus singing of prayers accompanied by rhythmic sounds of various instruments, at the end of any ritual, prayer, or '*Yagna*' (sacrifice) is the key to merging the mind, the wind, and the sky to enter the holistic '*Nirguna*' state.

10.1 Vastu Aspect of Some Religious Places

Temple architecture is a specialised subject in *Vastushastra*. Right from selection of site, to defining the dimensions of the structure, to placement of water source or pond and *deepmala*, to determining the exact form and proportions of the idol is a distinct science in itself. From *Vastu* point of view religious places of all faiths are of special importance, as devotees gather at these sites to offer their prayers and try to establish a link with the almighty. It is the meeting ground for the microcosm and the macrocosm. All religious places are built with due love and faith, but only a few locations cross the barrier of local fame and become prominent and well known throughout the land. Here, we have tried to understand importance of some of these places from *Vastushastra* angle.

10.1.1 Hazratbal (Islamic Religious Place in Kashmir)
Vastu Analysis:
1. North-South length is substantially greater than the East-West width.
2. Approach road is situated on the North side of the structure with central North entry.
3. Presence of a huge towering '*minaret*' in the Southwest zone.
4. Elevated South with pyramidal dome shaped roofing.
5. '*Kibla*' is situated on the West Side, i.e., the West zone is completely confined and closed.
6. Main ventilation is from the East Side.
7. The Northeast and East zones are blessed with huge water bodies having lunar shaped flow.

Vastu Virtues:
1. North-South length gives dynamic active quality to the space inside the structure.
2. Location of road on the North side and northern entrance give good financial stability to the Trust managing this religious place.
3. Towering minaret in the Southwest zone gives stability and peace to the site.

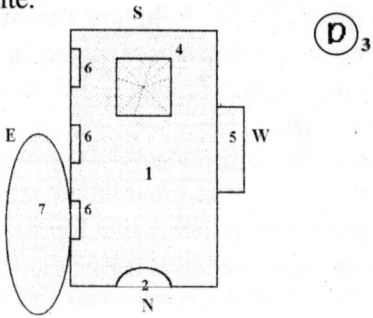

Plate 12: Hazratbal Shrine in Kashmir

Energy Concept in Temple Architecture 103

4. Elevated South gives majestic traditional values to this religious place.
5. Confined West zone deletes disturbances from the area.
6. East ventilation promotes *Pranik* energy flow in the space.
7. Location of water bodies in the Northeast and East zones create '*Ish*' stream and holistic environment in the space inside the structure.

Facts:
Throughout the turmoil and turbulence of Kashmir crisis sanctity of this religious place has never been breached. People of various religious faiths visit the place and enjoy the tranquillity and bliss.

10.1.2 Synagogue Lal-Deval in Pune
Vastu-Dosha in the Structure:
* East-West length greater than the North-South axis.
* East direction blocked by stone structure.
* A towering structure loads and obstructs the Northeast direction.
* Prominent Southwest and Northwest cuts observed.
* West side end of the structure terminates in a circular shape.

Plate 13: Synagogue Lal-Deval in Pune

Effects of the Vastu Deficiencies:
Although this synagogue is one of the most beautiful structures in Pune, there are hardly any visitors. No worthwhile ceremonies or religious meetings take place in this building, and it remains closed throughout the year for all practical purposes.

10.1.3 Haji Ali Dargah at Mumbai
The *Dargah* of Haji Pir at Mumbai is situated just off the seacoast. The main entrance to the site is from a causeway projecting into the sea from the South side. Access is from the overground path during low tide, and from an underground tunnel during high tide. Entry towards the main monument is also available from the North, East and West sides, which have openings towards the sea.

Water surrounds the monument at high tide. The semi-circular water-flow around the side is considered an excellent virtue in *Vastushastra*, and bestows the site with distinct eminence. The popularity of the *Dargah* can be gauged from the fact that it is bustling with believers from all religious faiths throughout the year.

10.1.4 Golden Temple at Amritsar
Devotees from all religious faiths visit the world-famous Golden Temple, the most important place of worship for the Sikh religion, and the seat of *Akal Takht*. The temple is encircled by water, which is considered auspicious in *Vastushastra*. The square foundation gives the place stability and strength. The cellars in the complex indicate strife and infighting. The entrance is from North side, bestowing the place with wealth and financial resources.

10.1.5 Basilica of Bom Jesus (Church in Old Goa)
In spite of the presence of other majestic and glorious churches with Venetian craftsmanship in its vicinity, Basilica of Bom Jesus is comparatively a widely known church in Goa. It is basically an example of Roman / Tuscan Doric architecture. The mortal remains of St Francis Xavier have been preserved here. People from all over India, Africa, and the Arabian Gulf assemble in this place during the novena and feast on December 3 every year and during special display for public every 10 years.

The South entrance is pointer to salvation from earthly bonds. The openings on the West give the place abundant wealth. Roads on East, South, and West sides of plot give it a businesslike character and prosperity. But the partly blocked North and East directions result in deserted look for the area for most part of the year.

10.1.6 Tryambakeshwar Temple at Nasik, Maharashtra

This temple dedicated to *Lord Shiva* in Tryambakeshwar form, has its North-South length greater than the East-West breadth. The West and Southwest sides of the temple are blocked by hillocks. A water pond is located on the Northeast side. All these parameters result in a virtuous *Vastu*. Despite the fact that this temple is located in a remote place and not easily accessible, people from all over Maharashtra visit this place in full faith and devotion.

10.1.7 Mahalaxmi Temple in Mumbai

The Mahalaxmi Temple in Mumbai is located along the seaside and is blessed with lunar shaped water flow along its periphery. Presence of such a water source is considered auspicious in *Vastushastra*, and gives the place fame, glory and financial strength. We find that people visit this Mandir throughout the year to offer their prayers. This Mandir is seen in all its glory and splendour during the *Navaratri* festival.

10.1.8 Kashi-Vishweshwar Temple at Varanasi

This temple is a classical example of construction based on *Vastushastra* principles. Its divine location on the banks of the river *Ganga* on the *ghats of Varanasi* has a distinguished character. The *Ganga*, the river of India the coming from, Northern Himalayas, flows eastwards along the *ghats*, bestowing the temple premises with bliss, religious éclat, reputation, and financial resources. The idol of *Lord Vishweshwara* faces thr East. The entrance from the East effects peace and tranquillity for the devotees in the inner precincts of the temple.

10.1.9 Lord Balaji Temple at Tirupati

The temple is located in hilly terrain and can be reached after putting in due efforts. The presence of solid rock on the South and Southwest side coupled with slopes towards the East and North blesses this site with virtuous qualities. The Northern entrance and a water pond on the Northeast side provided the Temple Trust with abundance of wealth and finances. It is perhaps the richest temple in India with millions of devotees coming for '*darshan*' every year.

Architecture and craftsmanship are relevant factors in the construction of religious places. But, only a few religious places appeal to peoples, sentiments and achieve distinction and glory. By design or otherwise some favourable *Vastu* aspects are found in all the famous religious places.

11. ARCHITECTURE TODAY - A VASTU VIEW

India, the motherland of the *Aryans*, has a rich heritage right from the ancient times. Only this land provides some form of continuity and roots for every single culture in this world. As per the nature's laws every ascent, after crossing a peak, is followed by descent. Same thing has happened to the Indian cultural and religious leadership. All the same, it is quite interesting to discover the beautiful way in which science and culture intermingled in ancient times to provide cosmic touch to the human life. Evidence of this pattern is available in several traditions and rituals practised even today. In the *Vedic* times science and art, seasons and rituals, traditions and culture all travelled hand in hand to develop the human mind as the ever-flowing essence of nature. It was a holistic endeavour with rhythm of intelligence and harmony of mind. Utility was just one aspect of this life, but not the only aim as seen in modern American culture.

In the 17th, the 18th and the 19th centuries, India unfortunately had to face rule by quaint people for whom trading was life, utility was tradition and counting coins was religion. These uncouth people destroyed the flow of Indian traditions. For new generations influenced by incorrect ideas of lifestyle, copying of Western customs has become the standard practice for their own version of cultural identity. In this cultural cyclone, many a good things in Indian tradition have started disappearing.

Now, we are in the midst of a completely degenerate and manipulative cultural scene. *Bhagavad-Gita* says that, "To enter somebody else's shelter is akin to death". We are witnessing the same phenomenon, more so, in the case of *Vastushastra*. In a way, the architects who have surrendered themselves to the Western culture and have borrowed ideas not suitable for the tropical environments should take the major share of the blame for this scenario.

11.1 Vastushastra and Modern Architecture

Modern architecture as taught in India borrows heavily from the West European architecture which has at its base total utilitarian view of life, and superficially draws sustenance from concepts like balance, harmony, rhythm, form, shape, proportion, functional utility, efficiency and beauty. These concepts are valid in *Vastushastra* also, but the inspirations differ. Certain important observations can be made as regards architecture being practised today, as against concepts found in ancient texts on *Vastushastra*.

11.1.1 The North Mark on a Drawing

Marking the North direction on a drawing has now become a mere ritual, without understanding its meaning or importance. The significance of the organic electromagnetic flux lines emanating from the North, is totally lost on the present day practitioners of architecture, who use North pointer for designating the roads and placement of plots. In ancient *Vastushastra* practice immense importance was given to alignment of the geometric axis of the Vastu and the geomagnetic axis. Hence, the North flow and the North marking were paid special attention in planning of a *Vastu*. The energetics of the *Vastu* is influenced by the North flow, as discussed elsewhere in the book.

11.1.2 Windows and Openings

In the tropical countries like India, the path of the sun is normally along the East, Southeast, South, and Southwest directions. For eight months in a year, we are directly exposed to the radiation of the sun. To avoid the malignant effects of solar radiation and to keep the house in shady cool zone, openings towards the South direction should normally be avoided. In ancient times this factor was given due consideration, and thickening of the walls on the South side and provision of entrances on the North side was a standard practice.

11.1.3 Water-bodies in the North/North-East Zones

In most of our ancient temples, a small lake of water or water body is always found in the Northeast zone. This practice has a scientific basis as far as dynamics of human mind are concerned. Since, study of science is not a pre-requisite for studying architecture; students of this discipline sometimes fail to understand the importance of a subject like energetics of a *Vastu*.

11.1.4 Avoiding roof slopes towards South, SW, and SE

It must be understood that the roofs sloping towards the South, Southwest, and Southeast project excessive area to solar radiation, leading to a very hot and unhealthy environment inside the dwelling.

11.1.5 East - the Direction of Pranik Flow

Wide openings towards the East direction always channelise the *Pranik* energy throughout the house. On the other hand, toilets and staircases in the East block the morning solar bliss.

It is a medically proven fact that sunlight is essential for life processes and the natural synthesis of vitamin 'D' in human body largely depends on absorption of sunlight through medium of skin. Further, *Yogashastra* maintains that early morning sunlight is a rejuvenator for the body. Ventilators and open spaces towards the East direction ensure that the entire household is exposed to the beneficial early morning sunlight for a maximum possible duration.

11.1.6 Avoiding Large Openings to the Southwest

In tropical countries, the direction of the wind is generally aligned to the West, Northwest, and Southwest directions. The Indian *Vastu* concepts dismiss the wind as a carrier of dust and believe in creating shadow regions for cooler homes that do not need wind for ventilation. By providing thick walls in the South direction and openings in the North direction, the houses are made thermal radiation-proof. The Western concept of providing ample ventilation from the West zone can only lead to spread of air-borne diseases through dust and pollutants.

11.1.7 Symmetry and Discipline in Forms

Least perimeter exposure to the sun and modular planning are the keys to *Vastu* concept. All fancy and unnatural forms are strictly avoided.

Most of India lies between the latitudes 9°N and 35°N. Between these latitudes, the surfaces that receive the maximum solar radiation, apart from the roof areas, are the Southeast, South and Southwest walls. The Northeast, North, and Northwest walls are less exposed. This implies that overall building form should be such that the exposure to the sun is minimised. This is possible in buildings with shorter North and South walls and larger East and West walls. *Vastushastra* principles expound that the length of North-South axis of a *Vastu* should be greater than the East-West axis.

11.1.8 Use of Local Materials in Construction

People, who live in the houses built from locally available materials, find a key to happiness through organic harmony and interrelationship between matter and energy spectrums. It rhythmically showers on the dwellers, a bliss of oneness with the surrounding nature.

People around the world are becoming aware about ecofriendly and environmentally healthy development. The word ecosystem has been commonly used for describing man and his environment. Ecosystem has been defined as, "any area of nature that includes living organisms and non-living substances interacting to produce an exchange of materials between the living and non-living parts". Environment can itself act as a source or a sink for natural resources, man-made products and by-products. In his search for exotic materials for construction and decoration, man has created pollutants which did not exist in nature and which cannot be disposed off by nature. By utilising local resources intelligently, it is possible to preserve the environment in a state of equilibrium and construct dwellings having maximum virtues as per *Vastu* principles.

11.2 Vastu Architecture

Architecture defines spaces and creates spatial forms in order to allot living spaces and utilitarian spaces amongst the occupants of a dwelling. Modern architecture sometimes gets so much obsessed with the ideas like economy, lifestyle, function, and efficiency that it almost forgets the inherent psychological needs like peace and tranquillity of a human being occupying the structure. Sometimes, the hands of an architect are forced because of professional compulsions like satisfying the demands of builders and developers. The individuality in architectural creations, visible in earlier times has in recent times been lost to problems associated with group or mass housing techniques.

Vastushastra deals with four kinds of spaces - space within human form, constructed space, terrestrial space, and cosmic space. A designer with *Vastushastra* insight achieves harmony between all these spaces, and in the process creates microcosm in the built-up space that replicates the qualities of the macrocosm. *Vastushastra* ideas result in design of houses, which are beneficial to the body and mind of the dweller.

In *Vastushastra* as well as modern architecture, the shapes like square and rectangle indicate safety, completeness and stability. But, the aesthetic shapes like triangle and rounded shapes representing grace and progress, which are popular in modern architecture, are avoided in *Vastushastra*. *Vastushastra* considers that the energetic space within a square or rectangular form create vibrations appropriate for peaceful and tranquil pattern of life.

Modern architecture, though outwardly elegant, is yet to imbibe the smooth way in which *Vastushastra* has found balance between symmetry and asymmetry in designing structures. But the trends are changing. Architects have started borrowing from concepts of climatology, environmental engineering, and cosmic energy flow principles to design dwellings that are in harmony with nature and closer to *Vastushastra* logic.

It is perplexing to note that *Vastushastra* and ancient cosmic *Mandala* diagrams are being dismissed in architectural seminars as mere tradition and memory architecture. Even after assuming that collective and personal memory plays a decisive role in an architectural layout, *Vastushastra* is far beyond this process. *Vastushastra* is a fountain of ideas and as such can be of great help during planning stage, construction stage, or finishing and decoration stage.

It is interesting to note that some Western scientists are promoting a concept of 'space therapy', which is based on the premise that well-defined built-up spaces have the virtuous ability to cure human body of ill health. The experiments have mostly been confined to pyramids and similar shapes. These ideas though rediscovered in the Western world are already available *Vastushastra* doctrines for interested and discerning researchers to tap. *Vastushastra* encompasses the whole cosmic existence, the microcosm and the macrocosm.

12. INDUSTRIAL STRUCTURES

Industrial structures need special attention in *Vastu* analysis. In an industrial environment, the human potential is exploited to its maximum in multidisciplinary activities - production clubbed with leadership function, research activity clubbed with market dynamics, achieving impedance-free movement of men and materials in crowded workplace etc. This balancing act needs a perfect understanding of contribution of each of the *Vastu* directions to the overall industrial space.

The Indian insight into *Vastu* planning is based on the concept of energy helix. This permits analysis of each part of the structure at individual level and then synthesising these into the total structure. *Vastushastra* considers a *Vastu* as a living being and as such, clubs the energetics of the *Vastu* with various parameters to make it lively. The character of a living entity is always reflected in its shape, form, size, and looks. Similarly, qualities like harmony and rhythm are part of a symmetric structure. In industrial structures, the contribution of various directions is analysed on the basis of form and shape of structure, as well as the plot.

Considering the *Jaivik* and *Pranik Urja* flow characteristics in an industrial structure, the following points can be noticed;

12.1 North Light Structures

The concept of 'North Light Structure' has been borrowed from Europe where temperatures remain within 15 degrees Celsius throughout the year. But, in tropical countries like India, most of the time the sun remains in the southern zone. Even in the '*Uttarayan*' (the winter solstice) the decline is hardly 10 degrees relative to the North. As such, the temperature differentials during the day exceed 15 to 30 degrees Celsius. In such a situation, projecting entire roof surface to the south to get northern light is an act of ignorance from environmental considerations. Due to high thermal absorption, such types of roofs disturb the entire electromagnetic field aligned with the structure. As per *Vastu* science, these structures tend to capture what is known as 'South Rhythm'. Case studies reveal that industrial units with these types of roofs suffer from low productivity and poor growth. All such structures need critical changes for achieving qualitative environmental enrichment.

12.2 North-South Length
If the North-South length of the industrial workshop is substantially larger than the East-West breadth, perimeter projected to solar radiation is minimised and results in cool healthy environment. *Vastushastra* maintains that all the activities follow an ordered and disciplined pattern if the North-South axis is greater than the East-West axis.

12.3 Work Environment for Executives and Staff
Vastushastra recommends that important executives should face the North direction with their sitting position in the Southwest zone. All the staff and workers should face East with their activity zone located in Central, Northern, or Eastern zones. From Vastu energetics point of view, Southwest zone represents the highest point of the helix, and decisions taken in the confines of Southwest zone flow without friction to lower boundaries of the structure. The North-facing executives benefit from eternal *Jaivik Urja* flow and properly tuned psyche. The staff and workers facing the East are aligned with the *Pranik Urja* flow, remain active due to ever-changing solar position.

12.4 Zoning of Industrial Activities
In an industrial undertaking multiple activities are taking place simultaneously. To achieve better co-ordination and cohesion in these activities, it is desirable that specific operations are restricted to definite zones on the basis of involved energy levels.

Activity	Zone
Research and development	Northeast
Heavy loads and activity	Southwest
Thermal activity	Southeast
Finished products	Northwest
Accounts and legal activity	East zone
Chief Executive's cabin	Southwest zone (south side)
Toilets/Canteen/Retiring Room	West zone

12.5 Landscaping and Loads

Landscaping plays an important role in providing cosmic envelope to the *Vastu*. Reshaping of a plot by landscaping is the simplest way to rectify the incorrect shapes and slopes in the plot. Remarkable improvement in the *Vastu* energetics results from the formation of external helix through load relocation in landscaping and planting of specific trees in landscaped gardens. In respiration process of the plants, rare gases are emitted, enriching the environment. This apart, the environment benefits from the plant biorhythm.

If any digging or excavation has taken place in Southwest, Southeast, or Northwest zones for locating underground vessels or water tanks or septic tank, this source of negative energy should be compensated by material loading at landscape stage.

Exposed water-bodies in the North or Northeast zones are abundant sources of organic energy, as the sunlight is polarised in transverse direction by these water surfaces. The Northeast zone lies in the solar shadow region resulting in low thermal activity, which endows this zone with natural quality of harmony as far as electromagnetic energy is concerned. The same quality is transmitted along with the polarised organic energy from the North and Northeast zones.

To reduce the extended Southeast related ill effects in some plots, water body in the Southeast zone is sometimes advisable.

A detailed analysis of landscaping is indicated in the case studies.

12.6 The Helix

It is said that life flows without friction and remains in natural rhythm if it is based on the logic of the 'Helix'. The helix form is followed right from the smallest virus to the gigantic 'Milky Way'. Most ancient scriptures refer to helix as the sacred curve. There are five different methods for implementing the 'helix' in a plot or a house, for effective *Vastushastra* remedies.

* Rhythmic compound or boundary along a plot for linking solar stream qualities to the ground profile.
* Landscaping and locating loads to peripheral zones of the plot to redefine the relationship between the ground and the structure.
* Varying levels in plinths as per the load characteristics of the *Vastu-kshetra* directions add to the vertical rhythm. The recommended pattern is as follows;

Northeast zone	lowest level
Southeast zone	level higher than NE zone
South zone	higher than SE zone
Southwest zone	higher than South zone

  One can attain helix in the plinth through this method.
* **Pattern of flooring** as per the requirements of the directions;
  * Marble in the Northeast, North, or East zone reflects the photon energy and maintains the East and the North as source directions of positive energy.
  * Agra red stone in the Southeast zone suits the thermal activity of the zone.
  * Yellow Jaisalmer or Marble or Shahabad stone matches the Southwest zone characteristics, as yellow colour represents '*Prithvi-Tatwa*', which has higher gravitational rhythm.
  * Kota or Tandoor stone may be used in the Northwest zone.
* **Colours:** As per '*Avak-Hada Chakra*', directions are classified on the basis of five great elements. A particular class of colours represents these elements. Hence, to Tree

enhance or reduce the specific qualities of Vastu direction under consideration, colour is the simplest possible tool.

12.7 Vastu Analysis for an Industrial Unit
General

Vastushastra is a science dealing with natural forces and energies, some directly experienced and some hidden. On the face of it, this discipline looks mysterious and ambiguous. But, all its rules and regulations can be traced to the basic sciences, particularly to the principles of physics pertaining to forces and energies.

Here we will present *Vastu* analysis for a typical industrial structure - buildings for a pharmaceutical manufacturing plant. For buildings housing medicine production facility, the concepts of quantum healing and energetics are of utmost importance. *Vastushastra* has immense scope in such cases to provide virtuous bliss of Nature to the whole production set-up.

Multiple paths are available for improving any given *Vastu*-situation. Here we are outlining the concepts and methodology involved in this process.

1. At the site, it is possible to offset any asymmetry by variations in landscaping, if the plot is of odd non-regular geometric shape.
    * By adjusting floor heights and plinths, it is possible to achieve harmony and rhythm suitable for the given ground profile.
    * Influencing the virtues and qualities of *Vastu* directions as per the *Vastu-Purush-Mandal* can compensate steep slopes in the ground terrain and odd shapes of the plot.
    * Planting of specific trees suited for *Vastu* directions can diminish the bad effects of incorrect eddy gradients in the plot.
    * Compound wall can be used to reshape the plot so as to achieve order and discipline in the site plans.
    * Cosmic environmental enrichment is feasible through structuring of length to width ratio of the plot nearer the Golden Ratio (1.000: 1.618).

2. Analysis of the energy-matter relationship can help in equalising slopes in the ground.
3. Landscaping and use of exposed water surfaces can attain cosmic helix in the building environment.
4. By reorienting and adjusting doors, windows and openings, it is possible to minimise surface exposure to the sun.
5. By blocking the *Pranik* energy flux through shadows and shades, the *Jaivik* electromagnetic flux can be enhanced to a certain degree.
6. Cosmic helix in the building environment can also be achieved through subtle use of materials, colours, and flooring.

12.7.1 Landscape Details (Fig.12.1)

To achieve harmony with nature and bliss in the surrounding environment, it is essential that a definite shape is given to the plot and it is aligned properly with the geomagnetic axis. For the plot under study, the following measures are recommended as per *Vastushastra*;

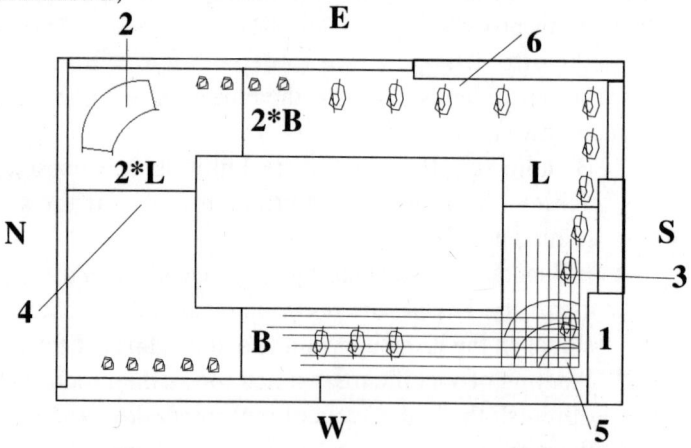

Fig.12.1: Sketch and Landscape Details of Industrial Plot

1. Provision of a heavy compound wall 24 inch thick and 7 ft high on Southwest zone, gradually reducing it to 18 inch thick and 5 ft high on Southeast side, and 9 inch thick - 3 ft high on the North and East sides. To match the shape, size, and periphery of '*Vastu-kshetra*' with the 'helix' pattern, these varying compound wall depths, widths, and heights

are very useful. The helical alignment of compound wall balances the vices and virtues related to *Vastu* directions and sub-directions.
2. Provision of marble finish lunar shaped water-pool in the Northeast corner, having outside perimeter 20 ft, inside perimeter 15 ft, and depth 5 ft. Circular water-body with diameter 8 ft and depth 3 ft can also be provided. The exposed water surface in the Northeast polarises the solar rays in transverse direction and thus, creating a source for ordered *Jaivik* energy.
3. Filling of pits in the Southwest, West, and South zones to attain ground slopes towards the North and East. This procedure offsets the energy-matter imbalance on account of heavy stress concentration in the Southwest zone. Elevating the Southwest zone in a *Vastu-kshetra* reorients the cosmic energy flow to simulate a cosmic energy helix in the environment.
4. The North and the East Side margins should be twice as much as those in the South and West.
5. Provision of heavy '*Gurutwa*' pedestal load in the Southwest corner of the plot. The aligned geomagnetic fields of a *Vastu* are disturbed due to high thermal activity in the Southwest zone. The disturbed energy fields can be balanced through heavy loads in this zone.
6. Planting of trees around the periphery of the property based on '*Vruksha-Vichar*'. Apart from the specific trees and plants indicated below, Audumber and Neem trees are to be planted on South side to provide humid environment that aids in environmental enrichment through reduction in temperatures.

East	Kuchla
Northeast	Khair, Velu
North	Pimpal
Northwest	Jayi
West	Arjun
South	Rui
Southeast	Moha

West/Northwest zone is governed by the great element *'Vayu'* and as such, planting of medicinal shrubs and Nilgiri on West gives aroma and bliss to entire *Vastu*.

7. Main buildings should be placed in the Southwest zone and aligned in such a manner that North-South axis of a building should match with the geomagnetic axis. The shape of the building should be rectangular.
8. Bore-well should be provided in the Northeast corner.
9. Septic tank should be located in the Northwest zone.
10. Provision of *pyramid*-like structures made of organic matter like bamboo or wood over Southwest passages. The dimensions of the pyramid could be 8-ft X 8-ft base and 3 ft height.

12.7.2 Internal Changes for the Vastu (Fig.12.2)

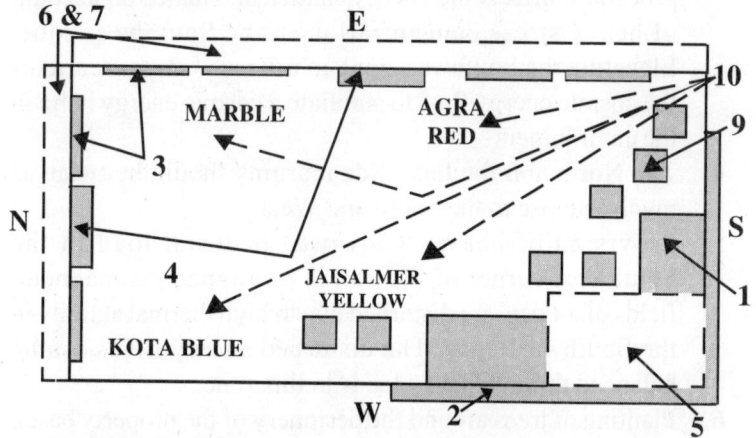

Fig.12.2: Schematic of Internal Changes as per Vastu Tenets

1. Provision of 18-inch thick wall in the Southwest zone. The South and West zones are exposed to intense solar radiation due to the Sun's East to Southeast to Southwest to West sojourn through the sky. Thicker Southwest walls act as shields against intense heat and keep the internal building areas cool.
2. Raising of the Southwest plinth by 6 inches. The Southwest zone is heavily loaded and or raised to compensate the imbalance in matter and energy due to heavy stress concentration.

3. Provision of maximum possible openings or ventilators in the North and East to maintain balanced Pranik and Jaivik energy flow through the Vastu.
4. Arranging East-side entry for the workers and North-side entry for the proprietors and executives.
5. Provision of additional floor in the Southwest zone. This helps in equalising the disturbed matter and energy balance in this zone on account of stress concentration.
6. Provision of slopes towards the North and the East. Sloping chajjas can be provided for this purpose.
7. Provision of terraces in the North and East, with levels in these zones lower than the South and West zones, to satisfy the concept of helix formation through level shifting.
8. Minimisation of openings and ventilators in the South and West zones. If openings in these zones are unavoidable, then tilted bay windows can be provided for simulating sunlight entry from the North and East. It is to be noted that source of light in the South implies that *Pranik* energy is in mutual opposition with North-South geomagnetic flux lines, which is a source of *Jaivik* energy.
9. Alignment of heavy machinery and heavy storage units in the South, Southwest, and West zones.
10. Provision of flooring to obtain the helix effect.

Northeast	White Marble
Southwest	Yellow Shahabad / Jaisalmer
Southeast	Pink or Red Agra
Northwest	Kota Stone

11. Painting scheme as per the well defined '*Ranga-Shastra*' principles in *Vastu* science. The colour variation based on five great elements and horoscope helps in attaining helix format in a *Vastu*.

Southwest	Yellow
Southeast	Pink or Red
Northeast	Glossy White
Northwest	Matt Finish Blue or Green

12. Placing of all light fittings and electrical points on the North and East sides.

The analytical approach adopted here has benefited the pharmaceutical unit immensely; in management-workers relationship and in smooth running of the plant at optimum levels. Taking recourse to *Vastu* principles at planning stage has distinct advantages - smooth progress of work and salubrious working conditions.

13. VASTU IN PRACTICE

In this chapter we will see practical application of *Vastu* principles in some specific cases. The *Vastu* analysis commences by first noting down the observations with regard to the directional aspects of a site, and then applying remedial measures to improve the virtues of the *Vastu*.

13.1. Office Site at Shivajinagar, Pune

Observations:
* *Vastu* has North-South length greater than East-West breadth.
* East Side and North Side are closed.
* Terrace towards South Side.
* Extended Southwest and extended Northwest zones.
* Entry from Southeast.

Rectification:
1. Effect of North-South length enhanced by cylindrical shell type roof made from Plaster of Paris, so as to match the stream characteristics with the natural geometry of space.
2. Extended Northwest and extended Southwest zones are treated by pyramidal roof to remove negativity of extensions.
3. Additional windows are suggested for the East and North sides.
4. Mirror to achieve extended Northeast zone and to simulate *Pranik* flow of East direction. The mirror should cover 25% area on the East wall.
5. To treat South terraces, cut-pyramids made of organic material are necessary.

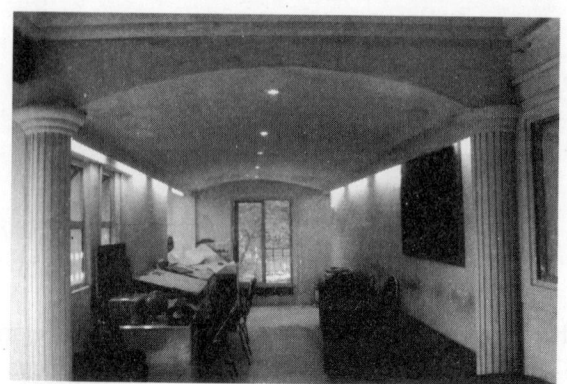

Plate 14: North-South virtue enhancement through cylindrical shell ceiling

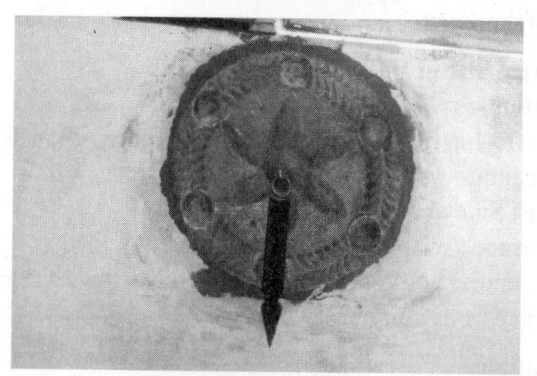

Plate 15: Lead disc with blue crystals for the West wall

Plate 16: Bhoumya Yantra and copper conducting plates for the South wall

Vastu in Practice

Standard Recommendations:
1. Lead disc with blue crystals on the West wall.
2. Copper mural with *Bhoumya Yantra* on the South wall.
3. *Ishanya Yantra* with crystal in the Northeast zone.
4. Jaisalmer Yellow stones flooring in the South zone with 10-cm additional level.
5. Stone sculpture in the Southwest corner.
6. Stone cladding on South wall.
7. Chief executive to face North and staff to face East.
8. All light points on the North and East walls.
9. Cabinet loads confined to South and West zones.

13.2. Warehousing Complex at Whitefields, Bangalore

Observations:
* The unit has North-South length for the plot and the building, with extension towards Northwest zone, giving 'L' shape to plot and building.
* A small cut on the Southeast zone of the plot.
* Extension to Northeast zone of the plot.
* Central North entry to the plot and Northeast entry for the building.
* Soak pit towards Northwest zone of the plot.
* Equal ventilation from East and the West sides.
* Staircase in the Central North zone, giving towering effect to the North zone.

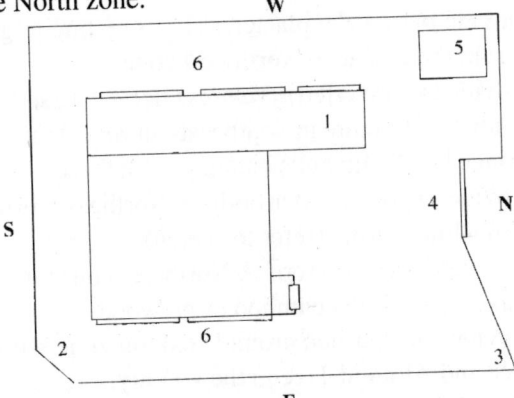

Plate 17: Plan modified as per Vastu for the warehousing complex

Vastu Reflections:
1. North-South length enhances the positivity of the building and the plot, and reflects immense capacity to compensate any *Vastu-doshas* present. But, extension to Northwest direction gives negativity as regards misplacement, disorganisation, and disagreement in dealing and disposal of material. Northwest extension leads to fears of theft, mismanagement, and labour problems.
2. Southeast cut gives rise to fear of accidents, fire, and lengthy complicated court cases.
3. Northeast extension gives good streams and improves blissful environment.
4. Central North entry to the plot gives good results, but Northeast building entry needs rectification through provision of additional central entry in the North zone.
5. Soak-pit towards Northwest zone is a proper position, but needs some rock garden on top to compensate excavated mass.
6. Equal ventilation from the East and West directions reduce the energetics of the *Vastu* and gives dullness to all activities.
7. Staircase in the Central North zone implies blockages in financial matters.

Recommendations:
1. Provide *pyramidal* plaster of Paris ceiling to ground floor area in the extended Northwest zone.
2. Provide two inverted *pyramids* (size 4-ft base X 8-ft height) in tubular structure in Southeast-cut zone. Place *pyramids* at terrace level with bells hanging from these.
3. Provide exposed water body to Northeast corner, cladded with white marble (refer to sketch).
4. Provide *pyramidal* roof to Northeast entry of the building. Make *pyramids* in bamboo or plywood.
5. Provide rock garden around soak pit zone with Christmas Tree and Almond Tree in the vicinity.
6. Close 50% ventilation on the West Side.

7. Provide bells in staircase zone with one chandelier in central staircase and small crystals with light on the landings.

13.3. Office Building, Bangalore
Observations:
* Property is South facing with entrances from the South and West.
* Property has North-South length.
* Property lies in the East zone of the plot with large site margin to West and minimum margin to East.
* Two roads from the Northeast and Northwest touch the plot.
* Main roads to the plot are from South and West sides.
* Toilets and pantries are in North / Northeast zone.
* Staircase in Northwest zone.
* Staircase is anticlockwise.
* North is loaded with terraces to South on the last floor level.
* Equal ventilation from the East and the West is available inside the office.
* Basement region has extended Southwest zone and cut in the Northwest zone.

Vastu Reflections:
1. For reinforcing the positive activity in the property, it needs treatment for reducing South and West streams.
2. North-South length is a good characteristic for compensating critical problems.
3. Large margins to the West and minimum margins to the East predict slow progress and disagreement in routine activities.
4. Northeast and Northwest roads compensate the South road.
5. Main roads from the South and West enhance the South stream, which leads to impediments and complications.
6. Toilets and pantries in North zone lead to sickness and dullness with complete failure in creative activities and projections.
7. Anticlockwise staircase gives incorrect biorhythms.
8. Loaded North and terraces to South give blockages in activities and financial losses.

9. To increase the East virtues, ventilation from the West should be limited.
10. Basement needs immediate treatment.

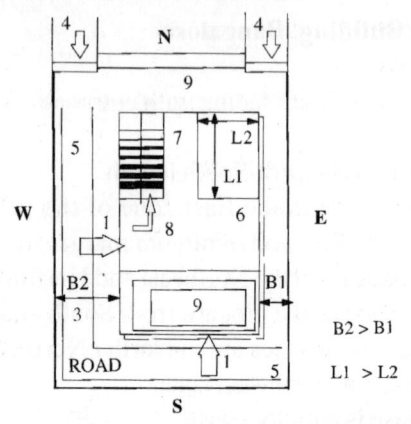

Plate 18: Plan as per Vastu for the office complex

Vastu Recommendations:
1. a) Provide 2-ft chhajja projection having *pyramidal* shape, over South and West Side windows. b) Use plants in South and West windows. c) Provide blue crystals in South and West windows.
2. a) Provide Almond and Christmas trees on extended West margins of the ground. b) Provide crystals, chandeliers, and bells in East zone to increase East stream. c) Provide mirrors on the East wall. d) Placing tray filled with water in the East Side window can also increase East streams.
3. a) Provide yellow shades of colour in the South zone. b) Provide stone claddings with 15% surface area in copper murals on the South wall.
4. a) Remove toilets from the North zone, if possible, and shift these to South, Southwest, West or Northwest zones. b) Provide mirrors, fountains, white lights, and crystals in the North zone. c) Remove pantry from the Northeast zone. d) Provide large windows on North walls. E) Marble flooring in North zone will improve North stream.

Vastu in Practice 129

5. Emboss clockwise designs on each step in metal or stone or colour to provide clockwise rhythm while climbing up.
6. Provide two inverted pyramids at terrace level on the north side parapet wall with bells mounted on cross bars.
7. Reduce the West ventilation by using cabinets, partitions, or curtains.
8. Extended Southwest zone in basement should be refilled with stones.

13.4. Site at Tungi, Lonavala
Geographical Layout:
* South zone is elevated with presence of big rocky hill.
* General contours show gradients towards the North, Northeast, and Northwest.
* Northeast zone is extended by upto 20% of the total area.
* Northwest zone is extended by upto 7.5% of the total area.
* Entrance to the property is from the South zone.
* A deep well is located in the Southeast zone.
* A big hilly portion is visible in the Southeast zone.
* Exposed water surface of dam is visible on the Northeast boundary.

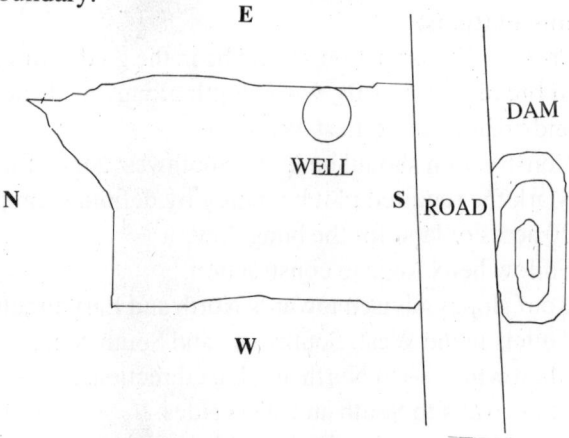

Plate 19: Geographical layout of the site

Vastushastra Reflections:
1. Elevated South eradicates the negative streams by curtailing the intense solar streams.
2. Slopes and gradients towards north and Northeast give acceleration to positive moon streams. Enhanced moon stream is natural bliss and holistic gift.
3. Extended Northeast zone represents divine sky full of positive events.
4. The marginally extended Northwest zone reflects a trend towards labour domination. But, excessive Northeast extension leads to a balanced situation.
5. Treatment of pyramids is needed on the South entrance/gate.
6. The well in the Southeast zone needs cover in the shape of a pyramid made of organic material like bamboo.
7. Loading in Southeast zone will minimise possibilities of failure in legal matters.
8. Exposed water surface in the Northeast zone will shower eternal polarised solar energy, leading to youthful zeal in all activities, and harmony of body, mind, and intellect.

Recommendations:
1. Proposed construction should be in the golden ratio (length to breadth: 1.5: 1.0), with length along North-South axis and breadth along East-West axis.
2. Construction should be in the Southwest zone of the plot.
3. Mark the required plot boundary by defining compound in 20 acres of land for the bungalow.
4. Follow helix logic in construction.
5. Roof slopes advised towards North and East directions.
6. Toilets in the West, Southwest, and South zones.
7. Main windows to North and East directions.
8. Stone walls to South and West sides.

The four case studies discussed here illustrate the practical applications of *Vastu* principles. *Vastushastra* always provides a better insight into worthwhile utilisation of user areas whether any construction is planned, or a project is under construction, or whether any premises have already been occupied.

14. NATURE, MACROWORLD, AND VASTUSHASTRA RULES

Indian *Darshanshastra* describes the life span of the nature in terms of four eons - *Krita, Satya, Dwapar,* and *Kali*. The nature has tendency towards progressive disintegration. *Darshanshastra* principles state that the nature attains plurality of destructive properties with every new eon, and moves towards self-dissolution. The nature embodying trinity of virtues - *sattva, rajas,* and *tamas* - is destroyed through over-dose of *tamas*. All religions accept and propagate the fact that the existence of life is a process of creation, preservation, and destruction. The *Bhagwad Puranas* give many instances detailing this process. This principle of religious origin, though outwardly similar to Darwin's theory of evolution, differs from it on fundamental issues.

The Indian mythological ages - *Krita, Satya, Dwapar,* and *Kali* - are in fact are accounts of rise and fall of virtuous qualities through various periods of history of life. Considering these aspects, the validity of *Vastushastra* rules can easily be traced to the laws of nature itself.

The wealth, the truth, the religious adherence, the cruelty, the abnormalities, the poverty, the famine - all these factors can be easily be correlated with the *Vastushastra* rules as applied to the directional aspects evident in various era. The two guiding principles; (1) relative heaviness of the South direction, and (2) location of the water in the North can explain the modalities of these relationships.

In *Vastushastra*, the North and the East directions are associated with divine qualities. The North and the East are the source directions for the *Jaivik* geomagnetic energy and the *Pranik* solar energy respectively. The smooth and free flow of these natural energy currents is traced to the qualities of the *Akash*

Tatva, the medium for event manifestation. Any interruptions or obstacles in the natural flow of these energy sources portend disintegration and destruction. Interestingly, even in the *Yogashastra*, all the auspicious and virtuous qualities of the *Chandra Nadi* are associated with the Northeast zone only.

As per the principles stated in the *Puranas*, we in fact can establish a link between the degeneration process in an era and the deficiencies or flaws in the qualitative aspects of the North and the East directions.

We present here different zone projections of the earth reflecting the influencing factors in each of the four eons.

In the eon *'Krita'*, the earth was on heavier side in the South with most of the landmass located in the South zone. Similarly, almost the entire North zone was under water. Over a period of time the Southern landmass started shifting towards the North. The poles of the earth shift by 1 minute of an arc every 100 years. As per the present scientific predictions, the North and the South poles are likely to interchange their positions in about a million years.

The scientifically analyzed movement of the continents towards the North and flooding of the Southern landmass can be interpreted in terms of the violent end prophesied for the *'Kali Yuga'*.

Vastushastra considers the combination of location of water in the South and massive North zone as pointer towards total destruction, while *Yogashastra* says that cruel and violent acts can result from the influence of the *Surya Nadi* which circulates within the confines of the South zone. The *'Kali Yuga'* will come to an end after the major landmass of the earth has accumulated in the North zone. At the same time, the interchange of the North and South poles will herald beginning of a new era.

14.1 Past and Future 50 Years for India as per Vastushastra

The principles of *Vastu-Jyotisha* permit analysis of planetary influence on a *Vastu* in terms of the natural horoscope. Though Vastushastra rules are applicable to the *Vastu* at all times, correlating the specific directions and planets allows interpretation in terms of definite periods of time and the events.

Nature, Macroworld, and Vastushastra Rules 133

India - Next Fifty Years

IV (N-W) MOON	III (NORTH) JUPITER	II (N-E) KETU
V (WEST) SATURN		I (EAST) SUN
VI (S-W) RAHU	VII (SOUTH) MARS	VIII (S-E) VENUS

Fig.14.1: Directions and planetary considerations
in Vastu-Jyotish of India

The cyclic nature of worldly processes finds relevance in correlating sequence of events in the past and deficiencies or '*doshas*' in the *Vastu* associated with a given event. A pattern can then be established pinpointing event series as related to the *Vastu-doshas*.

The above idea can further be elaborated by considering a specific example in which the year 1947 has been considered as the birth year of India. In the Indian tradition a period of 12 years or '*Tapa*' has its own importance. Since duration of 12 years is sufficiently long for predicting national fortunes, we can safely consider a period of 100 years for analysing cyclic nature of events.

Period	Defining Properties Planet		Aspecting
1947 - 1959	I	East character	Sun
1960 - 1972	II	North-East character	Ketu
1973 - 1985	III	North character	Jupiter
1986 - 2001	IV	North-West character	Moon
2002 - 2014	V	West character	Saturn
2015 - 2027	VI	South-West character	Rahu
2028 - 2040	VII	South character	Mars
2041 - 2053	VIII	South-East character	Venus

Table 14.1: Planetary twelve-year cycles and India

The picture clarifies as we consider the major events during 1947 - 1997, the 50 years period of interest, and analyse the significance of these events in terms of directional deficiencies and planetary influence. This type of *Vastu-Jyotisha* analysis is an entirely new field and still under development. Prescribing a set of rules for this methodology will be possible only after event versus *Vastu-dosha* analysis is carried out and counter-checked by widening the sample base to include different nations and cultures.

The time duration considered in astrology for world events is extremely wide - sometimes missing the events by 20 - 25 years. During this period, changes are possible in a nation's geography. As such, experts in this field play extra safe while handling this discipline.

Applying the *Vastu-Jyotisha* guidelines, we can say that the years 1947 to 1959, for India, were influenced by the Sun, the lord of the East direction. The Eastern zone of India has a natural slope with major rivers like the Brahmaputra flowing through and merging with the ocean waters on the East coast. *Vastushastra* considers this to be a fortunate event. During this period India gave the world a leader like Pandit Jawaharlal Nehru, who provided a foothold for the Indian polity in world affairs by promoting the ideas of *Panchsheel* and non-alignment. Since the Eastern direction was full of fortuitous parameters, this Sun-period proved productive for India.

1960 - to 1972 can be considered to be a period of mixed fortunes for India. This period was predominantly influenced by *Ketu* ruling over the Northeast zone. The Northeast landmass of India is solid and massive with natural slopes running towards the Southwest. But it is also a fact that the Northeast is covered by ice and snow, giving the zone a character of relatively reduced density and weight - a benevolent fact from the *Vastushastra* point of view. *Ketu* initiates making and breaking, providing mixed fruits for any actions. During this period, India lost Tibet to China. India under the premiership of the late Shri Lal Bahadur Shastri did win a war against Pakistan, but lost tactical advantage. These years saw the rise of the late Smt Indira Gandhi whose leadership provided India with mixed fortunes.

For the years 1973 - 1985 India's fortunes were controlled by the North direction ruled by the planet Jupiter. There is rise towards the North compared to the Southern regions of India - a major flaw as per *Vastushastra*. The massive north landmass is the very reason why the territory of Kashmir lying at the North of India was never fully integrated into mainstream India. From 1947 itself, Kashmir has been provided with special constitutional status, and has maintained separate identity due to militancy and religious fundamentalism.

If we divide the 12 years 1973 - 1985 into 3 separate periods of 4 years each, we observe an increase in unfortunate and violent incidents with each period. Up to 1973, an active *Ketu* with North-East influence characterised by break and make situations saw India win the Bangladesh war and play a major role in establishing Bangladesh as a separate nation. But after 1973, there have been a series of calamitous incidents like the proclamation of emergency in 1975, manslaughter in some parts of India during 1978 - 1982, and the violent death of Smt Indira Gandhi in 1984. The influence of North ruling Jupiter was wasted during 1973 - 1985 due to *Vastushastra* proscribed conditions of heavy North and slope towards the South.

The years 1985 - 2001 seems to be a period of political uncertainty, reflecting the frivolous character of the Northwest direction ruled by the Moon. The great element wind is identified with the direction Northwest. In the Indian context, the vacillating characteristic of the element wind can be seen in several incidents — short-lived Rajiv Gandhi rule, the violent assassination of Rajiv Gandhi, the stable but controversial rule of Narasimha Rao, frequent mid-term elections, etc. The Northwest province of India slopes slightly towards the Central Indian plateau and has a slight 'cut' in *Vastushastra* terms. All this has resulted in disastrous results for the nation-state and its political stability.

The period 2002 - 2014 will have a strong West direction characteristic determined by the powerful planet *Saturn*. Saturn is considered to be a hard taskmaster and a stubborn judge. A disturbed Saturn can bring to knees all the high-flying puerile characters. The Western zone of India is mainly a coastal region sloping towards the South. The period will be a tough one for India with major political and economic scandals receiving widespread attention. The planet Saturn is also an indicator of abundance of petroleum products. In these 12 years, India will face a shortage of petroleum products. The nation will undergo traumatic experience through a series of earthquakes and volcanoes, and man-made calamities like rioting and arson. The phasing out of Saturn will bring about major disasters for India.

The years 2014 - 2026 will be under the influence of *Rahu* governing the Southwest direction. Since coastal waters constitute the South-West zone of India, Rahu is expected to provide gains and losses similar to those provided by Saturn, but with in a accentuated manner. Rahu is an indicator of coups with bloodbaths. *Rahu* is also associated with lower grade social strata. Violence and arson are expected to be the order of the day. Large population may be wiped out through air pollution and toxic gases.

Thereafter, *Mars* having control over the South direction will rule the next 12 years. This period is indicative of solid military leadership and iron hand discipline. If the situation so warrants, a dictator will emerge from this scene to bring to an end the entire chaotic political situation by the year 2042. Subsequent years under the influence of a prosperity endowing *Venus* and a political superiority provider Sun will see India emerge as leader of the nations in world affairs.

15. VASTUSHASTRA AND EVENT MANIFEST

Eastern methods of inquiry and research are based on three basic dimensions of existence, i.e., physical, psychological, and spiritual. Every psychologically specific quality entails its own chemical and physical order. Mutually interdependent relationship of different systems is the basic concept in Eastern philosophy and logic. Comprehensive perception of nature without any constrictions of a biased analytical mind is the instrument of inquiry in Eastern systems.

Contrary to our self-imposed conditioning we find that nature is a continuum in which the human body cannot be alienated from the cosmic existence. As Einstein had postulated, a field is a continuum of all the possible information states, rather than a model for charting space-time events. All the probable events as a function of time, can be found in the continuum itself. In the Indian context दिक्काल (*dikkal*), a spiritual connotation defines the mutual relationship of space and time. As the scriptures point out, "as is the microcosm so is the macrocosm, as is the atom so is the universe, as is the human body so is the cosmic body". बृहद् आरण्यक उपनिषद (*Brihad Aranyak Upanishad*) defines the mind as तेजस् द्रव्यम् (*Tejas Dravyam*). We now have come closer to identifying mind with a biophoton field.

As put aptly by author Deepak Chopra, "Physical events are simply an expression of non-physical events. These non-physical events are bits of energy and information emerging from energy fields". In other words, events and flow of energy in subtle forms are closely interrelated. *Vastushastra* is based on these very concepts of event manifest. Further, *Prana* and life can be viewed in terms of energy and events.

The theory of event manifest as in *Vastushastra* says that the sky is full of events. If a person locates himself in a flux of energy streams free of impedance, blockages, and friction, then the effect of *Prarabdha* (past-deeds) is substantially reduced and his life becomes full of positive events.

The symbolic *Vastu Purush Mandal* is based on two-stream theory. The constant North to South flux is called as *Jaivik* or organic stream, while the variable solar flux is named as *Pranik* stream. All the deities in the *Vastu Purush Mandal* reflect the positive and negative confluence of these streams. In a sense, the logic of positive and negative confluence determines the arrangement of windows, doors, openings, and wall in a *Vastu*.

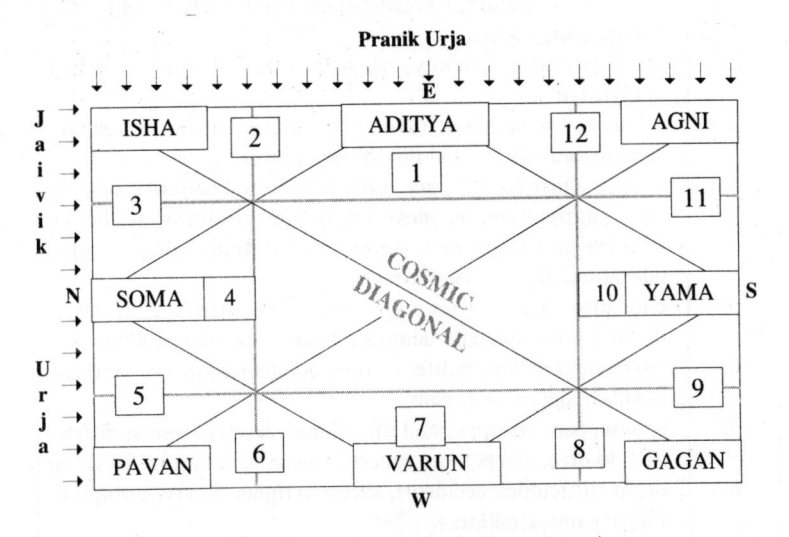

Fig.15.1: Vastu Purush Mandal

The North and East are termed source directions, while the South and West are known as sink directions. The laws of *Vastushastra* strive to maintain the basic character of these directions to attain holistic balance. The term '*Mandala*' is self-explanatory and represents the cyclic character of nature.

In *Yogashastra*, the East and North are directions of Moon streams representing happiness, bliss, grace, and space. The South and West are directions of Sun streams that characterise distractions, difficulties, violence, and voids. The same logic of creating the bliss of Moon streams and diminishing the sorrow of Sun streams is borrowed in Vastushastra. These streams play an important role at the building planning and construction stage also.

15.1 Astrology in Vastu Prognosis

Astrology plays an important role in the study and analysis of a *Vastu* situation. Direction related benign or ill effects of various houses in a horoscope are briefly summed up in the following chart.

House No.	Parameters under the Influence of the House in the Horoscope
1.	personality, nature, likes/dislikes, head, face, height, skin, colour, hair, rajyoga
2.	facial expressions, family, expenses, ancestral property, shares, knowledge
3.	relatives, brotherhood, travel, voice, music, literature, reading, writing, bravery, mental illness, will power
4.	spouse, close friends, pet animals, material benefits, vehicle, vastu, agriculture, business, know-how, neatness, aesthetics, flowers and fragrance, water related items, chest, higher education, degrees, Godliness
5.	education, degree, learning, culture, love, marriage, devotion, dreams, artist, art, entertainment, theatre, racing, gambling
6.	enemies, problems in life, sorrow, company, job, civil servant, stomach, digestive system
7.	spouse, partnership, sexual life, kidney, lasciviousness, married life, divorce, competitors, entertainment, art, court matters, war
8.	death, difficulties, accidents, ancestral rights, dowry, corruption, illegal gains, Godliness
9.	religion, higher education, temple, philosophy, progress, guru/guide, judge, court matters, vision, travel
10.	prestige, fame, promotion, rights, paternal backing, business, job, knee, head, sleeplessness, social and political life, rajyoga
11.	gains, gold, jewellery, fashion, clothes, circle of friends, returns, left ear
12.	loss of property, financial crisis, penalty, punishment, feet, moksha, sanyas, Godliness

Table 15.1: Significance of Various Houses in a Horoscope

In earlier chapters we have discussed specific cases for utilising astrological predictions in Vastushastra analysis.

A Case Study
In the following case we are using regression analysis to trace disasters encountered in life and their correlation with *Vastudosha*. This is a specific analytical study, and must not be generalised in any manner.

A renowned architect and builder had a flourishing business and opulent lifestyle with a fleet of car and a well decorated house and office. The moment this person shifted to a huge mansion with swimming pool on South and Southwest sides, he was trapped in a vortex of problems.

Within a year of shifting, this architect lost his only son in an accident. Within a couple of years he lost the control of his business and profession. At present he resides in a small rented house.

We will now try to correlate these events with *Vastushastra* logic. *Vastushastra* as deciphered in terms of astrology points out that, "Fault in South and Southwest zones of a *Vastu* are related to eighth and tenth houses of horoscope." The eighth house in horoscope represents heart, happiness and life of a son, while tenth house represents professional career and business success. With reference to the case in hand, we can easily see the relevance — severity of flaws in South and Southwest zones of a Vastu invariably leads to misfortunes.

Thus it is possible to match predictions from *Vastushastra* analysis with astrological projections. In most cases the results are surprisingly flawless. *Vastushastra* analysts can always refer to horoscopic conjectures to offer proper advice.

15.2 Vastushastra and Statistical Forecast
Let us now ascertain the effectiveness of *Vastushastra* forecasts as regards the breach of *Vastushastra* concepts and difficulties encountered at planning and construction of a building. We will use the proven laws of probability and statistics for this exercise.

We will first see two glaring examples, where failure to adhere to Vastu rules resulted in construction problems and litigation. These will then be correlated with statistical aspects of the case.

[A] It is interesting to observe a case involving demolition of a huge building in Kondhwa area by Pune Municipal Corporation. Not withstanding the fact that there were numerous unauthorised structures in this area, this particular building became the sole target. Cosmic energy balance, as per Eastern architectural concepts, was missing in this building and had five major deficiencies as per *Vastu* tenets. The demolished portion of the building was devoid of Moon streams and was under severe attack by Sun streams. These flaws can be listed as follows;

* South zone is placed at a depressed level over a sewer bed.
* The plot has extended Southwest zones with acute angle at Southwest corner.
* The plot tapers towards Southeast zone projecting a Southeast cut.
* The building is placed in the East and North zones with major site margins towards the South and the West.
* Centrally located swimming pool forcing slopes and lower levels towards the West zone.

[B] One of the building projects at Prabhat Road, Pune has some critical *Vastu* faults. Here, the entire load of the building emerges from *Vastu Nabhi* and structure itself is located in North and East zones. The South and West margins are comparatively larger than North and East margins. As per Astro-Vastu concepts, this type of construction points to court matters. Further, the building is placed in East zone with excessive West margins leads to disagreement and defamation in every walk of life.

As a matter of fact, the construction has become a subject of litigation.

Vastu Logic

Hardly 0.1% of plots are triangular in shape as per a general survey. As per *Vastushastra* such plots do not lead to any positive activity. We ourselves have observed two odd shaped plots where on account of substandard casting method and resultant reduction in concrete strength, structures had to be demolished. In construction industry, the probability of removal of slabs due to poor concrete strength is around 0.1%. Thus any failure due to simultaneous combination of these parameters should be (0.1/100) * (0.1/100), i.e., 0.0001%. *Vastushastra* forecasts such low probability occurrences with a great degree of accuracy, and confirms to the statement "Physical events are expressions of non-physical events." Ancient Indian sciences have a way of interpreting these non-physical events.

Thus *Vastushastra* not only solves personal equations, but points towards likely flaws in any major construction exercise.

16. GLIMPSES OF TRADITIONAL VASTUSHASTRA

Traditional *Vastushastra* is based on energy needs of a particular class of people. It indicates the specific directional zones suitable for habitation by various groups. This segmentation is derived from the qualities of eight directions, which are characterised by certain energy levels, and specific virtues as explained in the *Vastu Purush Mandal*. This logic has been extended in classification of sectors to be used for residence by various castes, creeds, and social groups.

Intellectual congruities are directly correlated with and are dependent on the daily routine. Energy needs of a given class of people do not remain static or constant over a period of time. Hence, in an ideal town planning, houses of various classes should be arranged as per their immediate energy needs. This apart, each class is found to have different eating habits and corresponding cooking methods. For planning purposes, these factors are given due consideration in traditional *Vastushastra*.

Constraints on financial resources of different classes impose limitations on choice of materials for house building, a factor reflected in traditional style of architecture. In ancient texts, the word *Vastu* is generally used for land or a plot. In planning a city or a town, logic of *Vastu Purush Mandal*, extrapolated several times over, has to be applied on the basis of energy requirements of different strata of society. Here, the *Vastu-Purush-Mandal* logic is applied first on a larger scale to demarcate public places, open grounds, schools, and residential areas as dictated by the virtues of different directions. Then it is reapplied on a smaller scale for separate plots to establish miniature figure of *Vastu Purush* in each case. Thus an individual gets associated with the nature, and microcosm is correlated with macrocosm.

It must be emphasised here that the caste factor in traditional *Vastushastra* points to vocation of a class of people rather than the narrow-minded concepts of caste prevalent in socio-political scene in India.

Methods of Vastu Classification

Three different methods are traditionally used for characterising a *Vastu*. To represent the effect of five great elements and the variation of energy spectrum, the cuts or squares used in conventional Vastushastra are either 10 X 10, or 9 X 9, or 8 X 8 type. Suitable nomenclature, generally a deity or a demon, is appended to these squares as per the type, form, intensity, and effective energy format. The charts include directional details, names of deities etc., and are self-explanatory.

Vastu-Purush-Mandal	Matrix	Vastu Type
Chatushashtipad	8 X 8	Housing colony layouts, planning of small townships, government or military camps
Ekashitipad	9 X 9	Houses of different classes of society, palaces, public places, government offices
Shatpad	10 X 10	Tall buildings, mansions, temples, auditoriums etc.

Table 16.1: Application of Shatpad Vastu, Ekashitipad Vastu, and Chatushashtipad Vastu Concepts

A *Vastu-Purush-Mandal* with 8 X 8 = 64 squares is useful in planning of colony layouts and smaller townships.

NORTH

NAG SHOSH	NAG	MUKH YA	BHAL LAT	SOM	CHA RAK	ADITI	ADITI PARJ ANYA
SHOSH	RUD RA	MUKH YA	BHAL LAT	SOM	CHA RAK	APA VAT SA	PARJ ANYA
ASUR	ASUR	YAKS HMA	PRIT HVI	DHA R	AAP	JAYA NAT	JAYA NTA
JALES HWAR	JALES HWAR	MIT RA	BRAH MA	BRAH MA	ARY	MAHE NDRA	MAHE NDRA
PUSH PADA NTA	PUSH PADA NTA	MIT RA	BRAH MA	BRAH MA	AMA	RAVI	RAVI
SUJ RIVA	SUJ RIVA	JAYA	VI SW	VA AN	SAVI TRU	SAT YA	SAT YA
DOUV ARIK	INDRA	GAN DHA RVA	YAMA	GRAIHA KSHA TA	VITA THA	SAVI TRU	BHRU SHA
DOUV ARIK BHRU NGA	BHRU NGA RAJ	GAN DHA RVA	YAMA	GRIHA KSHA TA	VITA THA	POO SHA	BHRU SHA POO SHA

SOUTH

Fig.16.1: Chatushashtipad Vastu Matrix of 8 X 8 squares

Vastu-Purush-Mandal with 9 X 9 = 81 squares is used in town planning for classifying locations as per the caste factor.

Glimpses of Traditional Vastushastra 147

N-W   **NORTH**   **N-E**

ROG	NAG	MUKH YA	BHAL LAT	SOM	CHA RAK	ADITI	DITI	SHI KHI
PAPA YAKS HMA	RUD RA	MUKH YA	PRITH VI DHAR	PRITH VI DHAR	PRITH VI DHAR	ADITI	AAP	PARJ ANYA
SHOSH	SHOSH	RUD RA JAYA	PRITH VI DHAR	PRITH VI DHAR	PRITH VI DHAR	APP VATSA	JAY ANT	JAY ANT
ASUR	MIT RA	MIT RA	BRAH MA	BRAH MA	BRAH MA	ARYA MA	ARYA MA	MAHE NDRA
VARU NA	MIT RA	MIT RA	BRAH MA	BRAH MA	BRAH MA	ARYA MA	ARYA MA	RAVI
PUSH PADA NTA	MIT RA	MIT RA	BRAH MA	BRAH MA	BRAH MA	ARYA MA	ARYA MA	SAT YA
SUG RIVA	SUG RIVA	INDRA JAYA	VIVA SWAN	VIVA SWAN	VIVA SWAN	SAVI TRU	BHRU SHA	BHRU SHA
DOUV ARIK	INDRA	BHRU NGA RAJ	VIVA SWAN	VIVA SWAN	VIVA SWAN	VITA THA	SAVI TRU	NAB HA
PUTRA	MRI GA	BHRU NGA RAJ	GAN DHA RVA	YAMA	GRIHA KSHAT	VITA THA	POO SHA	ANIL

S-W   **SOUTH**   **S-E**

Fig.16.2: Ekashitipad Vastu Matrix of 9 X 9 squares

Mystic Science of Vastu

NORTH

ROG PAPA YAKS HMA	ROG	NAG	MUKH YA	BHAL LAT	SOM	CHA RAK	ADI TI	DITI	DITI AGNI
PAPA YARKA HMA	RUD RA	NAG	PRI	I	T	VI	ADI TI	APA VAT SA	AGNI
SHOSH	SHOSH	YARKS HMA	D	H	A	R	AAP	PARJ ANYA	PARJ ANYA
ASUR	MIT	RA	BR	A	H	MA	ARY	AMA	JAY ANT
JALES HWAR	MIT	RA	BR	A	H	MA	ARY	AMA	INDRA
PUSH PADA NTA	MIT	RA	BR	A	H	MA	ARY	AMA	RAVI
SUG RIVA	MIT	RA	BR	A	H	MA	ARY	AMA	SAT YA
DOUV ARIK	DOUV ARIK	JAYA	VI	VA	SWA	AN	SAVI TRU	BHRU SHA	BHRU SHA
PITRU GANA	INDRA	BHRU NGA RAJ	VI	VA	SWA	AN	POO SHA	SAVI TRU	NAB HA
PITRU GANA MRIGA	MRI GA	BHRU NGA RAJ	GAN DHA RVA	YAMA	GRIHA KSHA TA	VITA THA	POO SHA	ANIL	NAB HA ANIL

SOUTH

Fig.16.3: Shatpad Vastu Matrix of 10 X 10 squares

Glimpses of Traditional Vastushastra 149

Ekashitipad Vastu-Purush-Mandal (9 X 9 matrix) is also utilised in placement of houses for politicians, public places, courts, theatres etc.

A *Vastu-Purush-Mandal* with 10 X 10 = 100 squares is applied in planning of palaces, mansions, temples, and big auditoriums.

Figures 16.1, 16.2, and 16.3 indicate significance of these 8 X 8, 9 X 9, and 10 X 10 matrices for *Vastu-Purush-Mandal*.

Aura of Two Streams and Concept of Marma-Sthan

ज्ञात्वा सिरा: सानुसिराश्च नाडीर्वंशानुवंशानपि वास्तुदेहे । ।
यत्नेन ममार्णि फलानि चैषां वेधं त्यजेत् यस्तमुपैति नापत् । । ३७ । ।
---- (स.सू.अ.१२)

"Impedance at *Upmarmasthan* leads to disease. Impedance at *Marmasthan* leads to struggle. Impedance to stream lines leads to misfortune."

We have defined the life diagonal connecting the Northeast corner of the *Vastu-Purush-Mandal* to Southwest corner as the main channel of energy flow. This stream has to be made free of blockages and friction for a smooth flow of energy. The intersection of the two diagonals in the *Vastu-Purush-Mandal* creates confluence zones - *Sandhi* or *Anusandhi*. To allow free flow of energy, any construction or load is proscribed for certain points in traditional *Vastushastra*. These intersecting points refer to the *Marmasthan* or *Upmarmasthan*. Presence of column or tree or for that matter, any construction or load over these points create obstruction to natural free flow of energy stream and results in torque like stress concentration or hydraulic drag like movement in these areas. In these regions, negative convergence of *Jaivik* organic flow and *Pranik* solar flow produce critical situations characteristic of '*Yama*' deity lording over the South zone. Symbolically, the *Marma-sthan* points are placed at the head, mouth, heart, navel, and left/right chest centres of *Vastu-Purush* (Fig.16.4).

Two strings (Nadi or Rajju), two diagonals (Kone-sutra), intersecting points (Sandhi), and sub-intersection points (Anusandhi) are marked on the figure of *Vastu-Purush*. These pointers characteristically indicate the central stream region of energy channels.

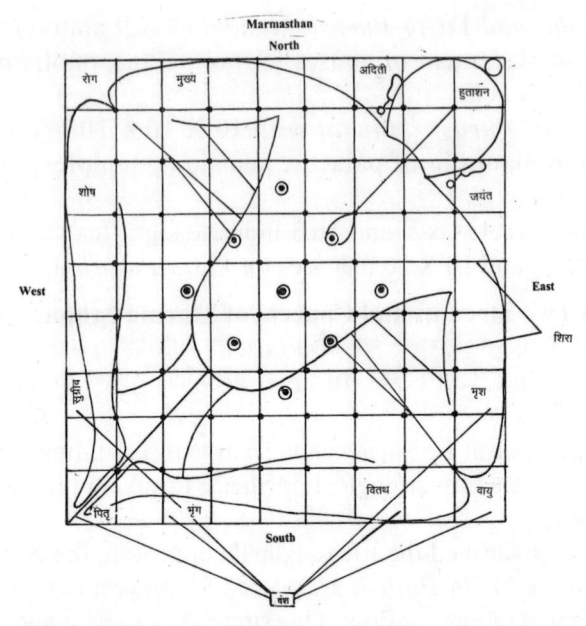

Fig.16.4: Marmasthan in Vastu-Purush-Mandal

Any type of construction or loading at these points disturbs the cosmic energy flow leading to turbulence, impedance, and resistance resulting in negative events and misfortunes.

Selection of Soil Characteristics (भूमिलक्षणम् Bhoomi Lakshanam)

In traditional *Vastushastra* we can find guidelines for demarcating colonies of specific population groups. Here, the suitability of certain soils for individual entities is decided on the basis of the biorhythmic and organic origin of a class of society. Characteristics of social classes are dependent on the nature of work or job normally pursued and exposure to the environment. Intellectual classes are hardly exposed to the scorching sun, while working classes rarely enjoy the cool and shadow regions. Traders work in a variable fluid environment reflecting the changeable nature of five great elements.

The holistic logic of soil selection is related to virtues of five great elements as projected by qualities of the soil. In *Vastu* texts, properties of soil or earth are described in terms of रूप (appearance), रस (taste), गंध (odour), शब्द (sound), वर्ण (colour),

Glimpses of Traditional Vastushastra 151

आकार (shape), स्पर्श (touch), and प्लवन (fall or slope of plot). These qualities find their equivalent attributes in human classes. Naturally, a correlation between soil characteristics and requirements of human groups can easily be established. It must be remembered that this classification is not based on any caste factor, but follows from the group occupation or nature of work.

As observed in मयमतम् *(Mayamatam): "It is the biorhythmic cosmic intelligence of different soils that fulfils the needs of different classes of people or reinforces the aura to suit their working environment."*

Intellectual Classes

For intellectual classes, a square plot in North zone is preferred. Audumber tree should be present on the plot and the soil should be white, representing Jal Tatva. Slopes towards the North direction are considered advantageous.

चतुरश्रं द्विजातीनां वस्तु श्वेतमतिनन्दितम् ।।
उदुम्बर द्रुमोपेत मुत्तर त्रवणं वरम् ।। १० ।। ---- (मयमतम्-अ.२)

It is to be understood that a square shape represents balanced qualities, and the white colour represents Jal Tatva defined as

।। आपो: ज्योति रसोऽमृतं ब्रह्म भूर्भुव: स्वरोऽम् ।।

Astrologically speaking, North zone is under the influence of Jupiter and Moon, which are the governing planets for education, culture, and religion. Hence, North zones should be reserved for intellectuals in any town planning.

Military and Police

For military and police personnel, rectangular plots in East zone are preferred. The soil should be reddish in colour, having bitter taste. The presence of *Pipal* tree on the plot with slopes towards the East is considered advantageous.

कषाय मधुरं सम्यक् कथितं तत् सुखप्रदम् ।
व्यासाष्टांशाधिकायाम् रक्तं लिक्तरसान्वितम् ।।१११।। --- (मयमतम्-अ.२)

Here, a rectangular shape represents strength and force, red colour represents *Agni Tatva*, and slope towards East leads to better correlation with qualities of planet Mars who is known as the warrior. *Pipal* tree symbolically exhibits the activity of *Vayu*

Tatva. All the above attributes and parameters are a must for military and police personnel.

Astrologically, the Sun and Mars having *Agni Tatva* qualities and characteristics of a warrior govern East zone. Hence, East zones should be reserved for military and police cadre in town planning.

Traders and Businessmen

A rectangular plot with excess length compared to width is preferred for traders and business class. The plot should be in Southern zone with yellow coloured soil having acidic taste. The plot should slope towards the East.

षडं शेनाधिकायामं पीतमम्ल रसान्वितम् ।

प्लक्षद्रुमयुतं पूर्वावनतं शुभदं विशाम् ।।१३।। ---- (मयमतम्-अ.२)

It is an acknowledged fact that excessive length in rectangular shape allows for better stream flow characteristics. The yellow colour simulates *Prithvi Tatva* symbolising stability, and the Eastward slope reinforces *Aditya Pravah*. This means that stability is achieved along with alacrity because of the favourable role played by the colour, the form, and the shape. These attributes are a prerequisite for a stable and a enhanced growth pattern for the business. Astrologically the tenth house in a horoscope represents business, profession, and work. Therefore, in town planning it is quite logical to reserve Southern zone for accommodating traders and businessmen.

Working Classes

Rectangular plot with length far in excess of width is preferred for housing of working classes. The soil should be black in colour and bitter in taste, with slopes towards East considered useful.

चतुरंशाधिकायामं वस्तु प्राक्प्रवणान्वितम् ।

कृष्णं तत् कटुकरसं न्यग्रोधद्रुम संयुतम् ।।१४।।   मयमतम् अ.३

Geologically black and bitter soil is rich in mineral contents, and can be suitably used for vegetation and plantation. Excessive length of a house can be used for constructing separate rooms to accommodate different activities which are part of daily routine of the working classes and need to be carried out without disturbing

Glimpses of Traditional Vastushastra 153

their work assignments. The task areas include storage place for grain, cattle sheds, poultry enclosures, workshop etc. Additionally the slope towards the East allows for *Aditya Pravah* inside the house.

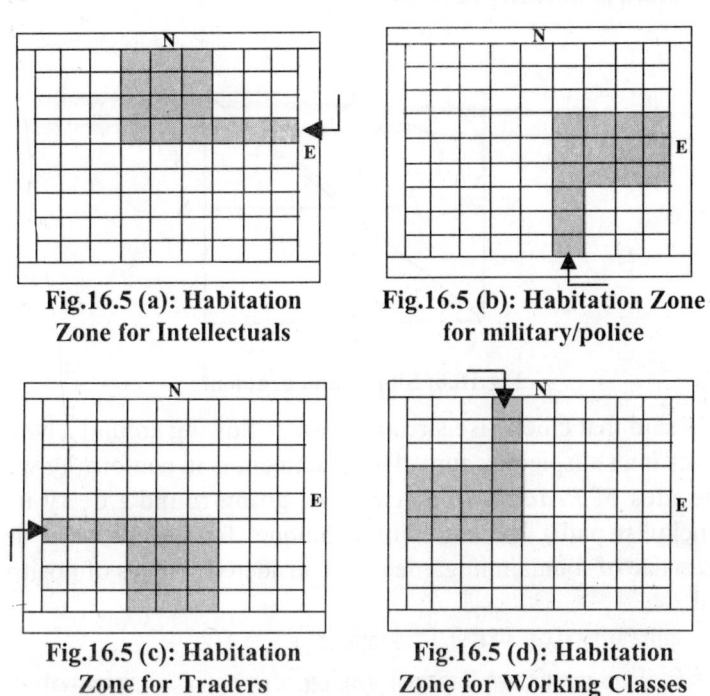

Fig.16.5 (a): Habitation Zone for Intellectuals

Fig.16.5 (b): Habitation Zone for military/police

Fig.16.5 (c): Habitation Zone for Traders

Fig.16.5 (d): Habitation Zone for Working Classes

Astrologically West zone is ruled by the planet Saturn, which represents working class activities. Hence in town planning it advisable to allot West zone for housing of the working classes.

Comments

देवानांतु द्विजातीनां चतुरश्रायताः श्रुताः ।
वस्त्वाकृतिरनिन्द्या सावाक्प्रत्यग्दिक्सूमुन्नता   मयमतम् अ.३

In Mayamatam, it is said that intellectuals can also use a rectangular plot with West and South sides duly loaded and at higher level. Slopes towards the East and North create natural positive cosmic moon streams, which can balance the aggressive character of the rectangular shape.

धवलं रक्तवर्णं च स्वर्ण-कृष्णं-कपोतकम् ।
षडश्रैश्च समायुक्ता सर्वसम्पन्प्रदा धरा ।।१६।। ----- मानसारम् अ.४

In this particular stanza from *Manasaram*, natural gradients of a plot are designated in terms of a helical order. We already have discussed about helix in earlier chapters.

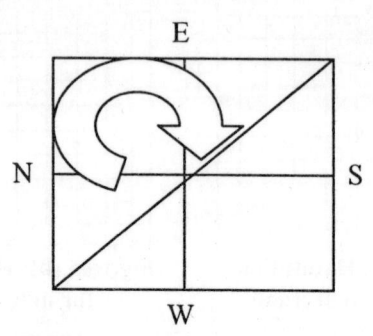

Fig.16.6: Slopes and gradients

It is said that clockwise stream of water flowing around a house gives it an auspicious aura. This statement is in conformity with the idea of *Pradakshina* (ritual of going round a deity in a clockwise path). In Feng Shui technique also flow of water and presence of fountain in garden are considered sources of positive qui.

कृमिवल्मीकरहिता निर्मूषी निष्कपालिनी ।
निरस्थि: सूक्तीसिकता रज्जुवर्जा शुभावहा ।।१८।। ----- मानसारम् अ.४

If a plot is free from attack by insects, rats, white ants, and if bones, skulls, conches, shells, snails, sand, and porous materials are absent in the soil, then qualities of a house built on such a plot are automatically elevated. Holistic environment cannot be established in a piece of land shaped like either turtleback or a circle or a triangle and having a hard surface. If two, three or four roads end on a plot of land, such a plot cannot give good results.

In effect this verse explains the physical, psychological, and divine constraints associated with a piece of land. Analysing further, we can say that in a turtleback shaped land, the central *Brahma* region is at a higher altitude leading to placement of *Vastu Nabhi* in an inverted position, which is indicative of diseased land as per *Vastu* concepts.

Glimpses of Traditional Vastushastra 155

श्रियं दाहं तथा मृत्युं धनहानिं सुतक्षयम् ।
प्रवासं धनलाभं च विद्यालाभं क्रमेण च ।
विदध्यार चिरेणैव पूर्वादिप्लववतो मही ।
मध्यप्लवा मही नेष्टा न शुभाप्लवतत्परा ।।

(बृहद् वास्तुमाला)

Here, gradients in various directions on a plot are correlated with various facets of human life.

Land sloping towards	Quality indicated
East	prosperity
Southeast	burning sensation
South	advent of death
Southwest	loss of wealth
West	loss of offspring
Northwest	instability
North	prosperity
Northeast	good education
Land hollow at centre	hardship in life

Table 16.2: Land Characteristics and Personal Fortunes

These are some of the pointers in relation to the characteristics of a piece of land. These are exactly reflected in *Vastu-dosha* prognostics derived from natural horoscope.

Similar verses are found in an old treatise on *Vastushastra*, "*Vishwakarma Prakash*".

भुष प्लवं प्रवक्ष्यामि नराणां च शुभाशुभम् ।
पूर्वप्लवा वृद्धिकरी ऊत्तरा धनदा स्मृतम् ।
अर्थक्षयकरी विद्यात् पश्चिम प्लवना ततः ।
दक्षिण प्लवना पृथ्वी नराणां मृतिदा भवे)
----- (वास्तुविद्या)

पूर्वप्लवे भवेलक्ष्मीं ----- (विश्वकर्मप्रकाश अ.२)
कालकृष्टे अथवा देशे ----- (मत्स्यपुराण अ. २५३)

The common theme running through all these verses points to the fact that human being shares a bond with his land through biorhythms and this bond serves as a blueprint for his growth and future. Biorhythms, intellectual congruities, and natural frequencies of objects are all interdependent phenomena. Quality relationships with biorhythms of the land influence the other two parameters of human consciousness in a positive manner. A land through its positive fertile characteristics establishes a definite relationship with plants. Similar relationship is evident in a plot of land and the human beings served by it.

In some *Vastu* related disciplines, water retention characteristics of the soil found in the plot and its compacting strength are correlated with human fortunes.

खाते सितादिमास्यानि ----- स.सू.पा. अ.८

There is a mystic method used for classifying land types. White, red, yellow, and black flowers are kept in a pit formed in the plot to find out the specific flowers in contact with the soil that attain superior qualities.

The colours in this system represent the five great elements, and their concurrent reference to class characteristics in society is used for classifying the land types suitable for intellectuals, business class, military and police personnel, and the working classes.

Different colours have specific aura and this effect can be suitably used in land selection, choice of construction materials, decoration etc. for the benefit of human beings.

Prangan Pravesh - Limiting the Immensity
A *Vastu* domain where characteristics of different directions find their proper space is created when we construct a compound wall.

The cardinal qualities and efficacy of directions can be achieved only if energy streams are properly channelled. This effect is possible through construction of a compound wall. While commencing a project, construction of a compound wall is a primary ritual in *Vastushastra*. This ceremony in effect activates the cosmic energies in the symbolic *Vastu-Purush*.

Zones and Entrances

We have seen earlier that specific zones of directions enhance positivity for particular classes of people. This correspondence can be summarised as below:

North zone	Intellectuals
East zone	Military and Police
South zone	Traders and Businessmen
West zone	Working Classes

It is easy to plan the spaces based on this logic, and *Vastu-Purush-Mandal* of a township. Once residential zones are fixed, it is a simple task to mark out the spaces for public utilities, recreation, and social activities.

North represents *Jal Tatwa*, which enhances intelligence through its basic nature pertaining to light and purity. East has qualities of Mars - leadership and solidity. A pattern emerging from this type of logic is utilised in establishing zones of habitation on the basis of class characteristics.

While deciding the main entrance to a plot, due care is taken to maintain clockwise rhythm in all movements. If a grid of 9 X 9 is specified directionwise for a particular class, right handed cyclic entrance is attained by moving to next forward direction in a clockwise pattern. Fig.17.6 explains this logic and provides the necessary information on permitted forward entrances. Extending the logic further, we can say that for any direction, the 4th house entry in the grid of 9 X 9 is the most logical one in the *Vastu-Purush-Mandal*. Entrance through any other square on the grid can create flaw either in the flow of *Jaivik* and *Pranik* streams or in the right-handedness of the scheme.

Once this logic of 4th square for entrance is finalised in the *Vastu-Purush-Mandal*, the main entrance to the plot cannot conform with direction of the main gate to the house, as we have to follow the principle of right-handed clockwise entry.

EAST

दु:खम्	शोक:	धनम्	नृप मान्यम्	महद् भयम्	त्रिजन्म	अपुत्रता	हानि:
शोक: प्राप्ति:							मरणम्
दु:खम्							वन्धनम्
प्राप्ति:							भीति
सुखा गम:							पुत्राप्ति:
संपत्ती: हानि:							धनागम् यशो लब्धि
महद् दु:खम्							चौरा भयम्
शवृद्धि:							व्याधि भीति
शोक:	दु:खम्	धन लाभ	सौ भाग्यम्	धनागम्	लक्ष्मी प्राप्ति:	त्रि दु:खम्	नि:स्वम्

Fig.16.7: Dwar Nivesh Phal

In case the entrance to the plot and entrance to the house match in any manner, then it implies that the failure of the logic of 4th house entry in the 9 X 9 grid of *Vastu-Purush-Mandal*. This can create disorder for the plot or for the dwelling. Classically this disturbance due to correspondence between the gates of the plot and the house is called as *Utsang*. On the basis of directional properties and the natural horoscope, *Utsang* indicates negative results.

For determining favourable direction and position of main door of a dwelling, *Dwar Nivesh Phal* is a useful guide. The much-maligned South direction provides three positive locations for placing the main door, while the popular East direction allows only two positions for locating the entrance. Contrary to the popular belief, entrance can be located at any direction, provided it subscribes to the logic of 9 X 9 grid and clockwise access.

In this chapter we discussed the some classical concepts in traditional *Vastushastra*. The current trends in town-planning and mass housing projects draw heavily from Western techniques of architecture, not ideally suited for Indian conditions. Climatology is one topic in modern architecture, if followed in right spirit, can help in designing housing projects in conformity with patterns in traditional *Vastushastra*.

17. VASTUSHASTRA GUIDELINES

After analysing the *Vastushastra* tenets and principles, some ground rules can be formulated for deriving optimum benefits from *Vastu-Vidya* at the planning stage itself.

17.1 Before Planning a Vastu

The following guidelines if interpreted and applied in the right spirit, can help in planning and designing a virtuous Vastu.

1. Geometric axis of the *Vastu* should be aligned to match with the geomagnetic axis of the plot.
2. The North-South axis should be longer than the East-West axis.
3. The major part of the *Vastu* construction should be located in the Southwest zone of the plot and open spaces should be provided in the Northeast direction.
4. Underground water tanks should be planned in the North and the Northeast directions.
5. Ground terrain should have gradual slopes towards the North and the East directions.
6. Lumber room or storage room should be located in the Southwest corner.
7. Excavation should commence from the Northeast side and move in a clockwise direction towards the Southeast side and then onto the Southwest direction. Activities like providing a footing for the structure and ground filling must begin in the Southwest.
8. To avoid any ill effects of neighbouring *Vastu* and its domain, it is advisable to complete the construction of the entire compound wall before commencing any other construction activity. The South and the West side compounds should be of stone construction, solid and heavy, and with sufficient height.

9. Soil-analysis should be carried out. The soil not having requisite characteristics as per the *Vastushastra* should not be used for ground filling. Good quality soil should be procured from elsewhere, for this purpose.
10. A bore-well or a constructed well for a water source should be located in the North or the Northeast directions.
11. The Southern walls should not have any door or window openings. The wall in this direction should be either 18-inch (45-cm) thick construction or a double wall with cavity in-between.
12. Maximum possible number of doors, windows, and ventilators should be provided in the North, Northeast, and East directions.
13. In the same house, differential levels for internal rooms are not advisable.
14. Basements and cellars should be avoided.
15. Roofs, if provided, should have slopes towards the East, the Northeast, and the North directions.
16. Roofs slanting towards the South and the West directions are not advisable.
17. If possible, an additional room or a floor should be constructed on the Southwest side.
18. Extra height should be allowed for parapet walls on the South and the West sides.
19. The Southwest plinth level should be 9 inches (22.5 cm) higher than the other plinth levels and the planned ground slopes towards the North and East directions should be taken into consideration before determining the other construction levels.
20. Audumber family trees should be planted on the South border, while the West side could have Nilgiri (Eucalyptus) trees or medicinal, herbal, and aromatic plants and bushes.
21. The North and the East sides should be provided with open spaces for free air circulation.
22. In cases where the neighbouring plot includes a water-body or pond on its Northeast side, the height of the compound

wall on the Southwest side of one's own plot should be raised sufficiently to make the Southwest side extra massive. This provision can be made at the landscaping stage itself.

23. It is considered profitable to purchase additional adjoining land on the North, Northeast, and East sides. On no account any land should be acquired on the South or West sides, once a house has been constructed on a plot.

24. In construction of the structure proper, uneven shapes, fancy windows and unwarranted cantilever projections should strictly be avoided.

25. In ownership flats, options for prior planning are limited. Hence, the *Vastu* should be made healthy and full of vitality through external means. Selection of a painting scheme for the flat based on the *Shri Ranga Chakra* in such cases proves very helpful.

26. Lightweight items should be placed in the North and the East directions, while rigid and heavy things should be located in the South and the West. This principle is applicable not only to the entire *Vastu*, but to individual rooms also.

27. If the East side is blocked on any account, additional windows should be provided in the North direction. If possible, the sunlight should be beamed in from the East direction by making use of some sort of reflector mechanism.

28. The North, Northeast, and East side walls should be decorated preferably with photographic frames or paintings of Goddesses and wall papers with natural scenery etc.

29. The North, Northeast and East side walls should be painted with bright glossy colours, while the painting scheme for the West and South side walls could use dull, matt-finish type colours.

30. Toilets should be located in the South and the West.

31. A *Vastu* with 100% matching of characteristics and performance as espoused in *Vastushastra* is an idealistic

condition. In practice, it is absolutely necessary or sometimes, even sufficient to achieve minimum of 50% to 60% of the characteristics of the ideal conditions in a Vastu.

32. Overhead tank should be on the West side. A tank on the North or the East side is also permissible. But, underground or ground level water should never be stored in the West or the Southwest directions.
33. One should sleep with his head pointing towards the East* or the South direction. Beds should be arranged accordingly. (*as per ancient texts on Vastu Vidya)
34. *Puja-room* (prayer room) should be planned in such a manner that the back of the Goddesses should touch the East side wall, with the person facing the East direction while performing the puja.
35. Multi-coloured fancy lamps should be fixed on the North and the East walls, specifically avoiding the South side surfaces.
36. If possible, the *Vastu* should be extended by 4 - 5 ft (1.5 mtrs) in the Northeast direction to ensure the Northeast directional bliss for the household or a shop.

17.2 Vastu-kshetra Analysis through Vastu-Jyotisha

Applying *Vastu* rules becomes an easier task if *Vastu-kshetra* or a plot of land is subjected to thorough inspection. Apart from the *Bhoomi Lakshanam* concepts from ancient texts on *Vastushastra*, an analytical approach based on Vastu-Jyotisha can always suggest better solutions for improving qualities of a *Vastu*, at a planning stage itself. The following charts summarise the concepts of *Vastu-Jyotish* in terms *Vastu-dosha* arising out of cut or extension to a plot.

Horoscope projection indicated here follows North Indian pattern. Only the primary effects of houses have been considered here. The influence of exaltation or debilitation of planets, the strength of a planet in a given house, yogas etc. have also to be analysed for a comprehensive picture regarding *Vastu* situation.

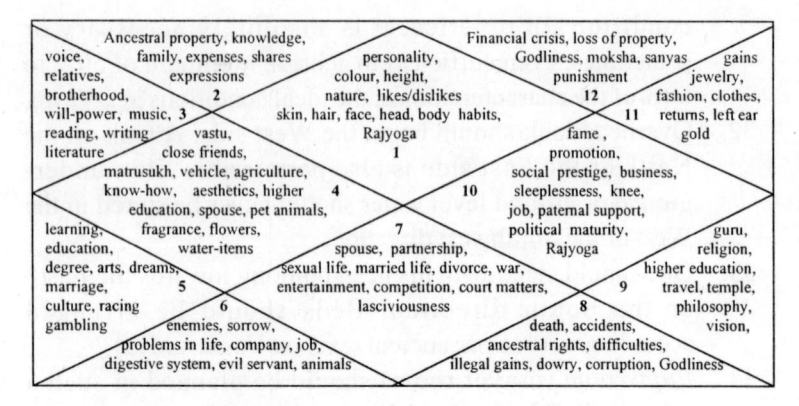

```
                Ancestral property, knowledge,              Financial crisis, loss of property,
  voice,        family, expenses, shares      personality,    Godliness, moksha, sanyas    gains
  relatives,    expressions                   colour, height,   punishment                 jewelry,
  brotherhood,          2                     nature, likes/dislikes       12              fashion, clothes,
  will-power, music, 3                        skin, hair, face, head, body habits,   11    returns, left ear
  reading, writing      vastu,                       Rajyoga              fame ,           gold
  literature            close friends,                  1                 promotion,
                matrusukh, vehicle, agriculture,                       social prestige, business,
                know-how,  aesthetics, higher  4          10          sleeplessness, knee,
                education, spouse, pet animals,                       job, paternal support,
  learning,     fragrance, flowers,                 7                 political maturity,        guru,
  education,            water-items                                         Rajyoga              religion,
  degree, arts, dreams,              spouse, partnership,                                  higher education,
  marriage,     5               sexual life, married life, divorce, war,             9     travel, temple,
  culture, racing                entertainment, competition, court matters,                philosophy,
  gambling          6                    lasciviousness            8                        vision,
                enemies, sorrow,                                death, accidents,
                problems in life, company, job,                ancestral rights, difficulties,
                digestive system, evil servant, animals     illegal gains, dowry, corruption, Godliness
```

Fig.17.1: Horoscope Projection in North Indian Style

The task of understanding a complex Vastu case is simplified through judicious use of astrology. Once the strengths and weaknesses of a Vastu Kshetra (plot) and Vastu are comprehended, effective remedial actions can easily be devised. In the following charts shape of a plot is interpreted in terms of its relationship with particular houses in natural horoscope. Further, these houses give potent effects according to enhancement or debilitation of their virtues.

Vastushastra Guidelines 165

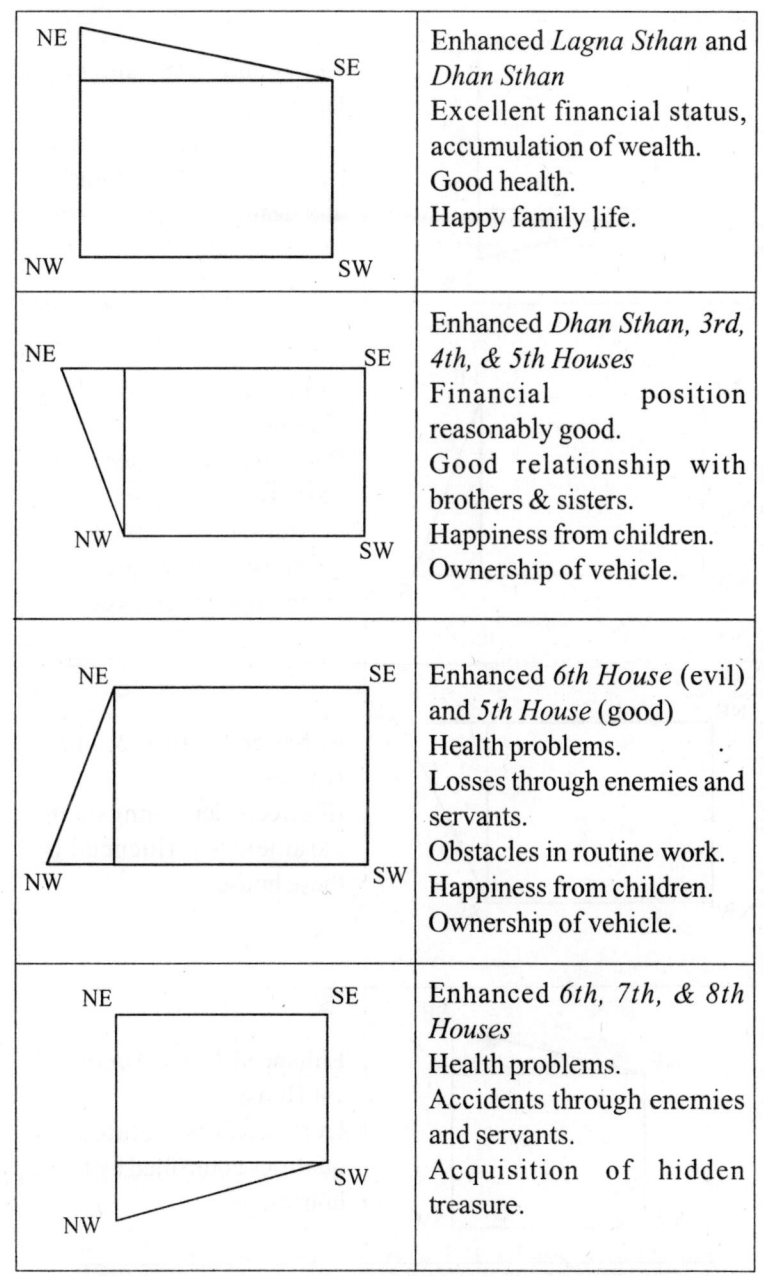

Plot Shape	Astrological Significance
NE / SE / NW / SW (extended NE-SE top)	Enhanced *Lagna Sthan* and *Dhan Sthan* Excellent financial status, accumulation of wealth. Good health. Happy family life.
NE / SE / NW / SW (extended NW side)	Enhanced *Dhan Sthan, 3rd, 4th, & 5th Houses* Financial position reasonably good. Good relationship with brothers & sisters. Happiness from children. Ownership of vehicle.
NE / SE / NW / SW (extended NW corner)	Enhanced *6th House* (evil) and *5th House* (good) Health problems. Losses through enemies and servants. Obstacles in routine work. Happiness from children. Ownership of vehicle.
NE / SE / NW / SW (extended SW)	Enhanced *6th, 7th, & 8th Houses* Health problems. Accidents through enemies and servants. Acquisition of hidden treasure.

Fig.17.2: Shape of a Plot and Astrological Significance (I)

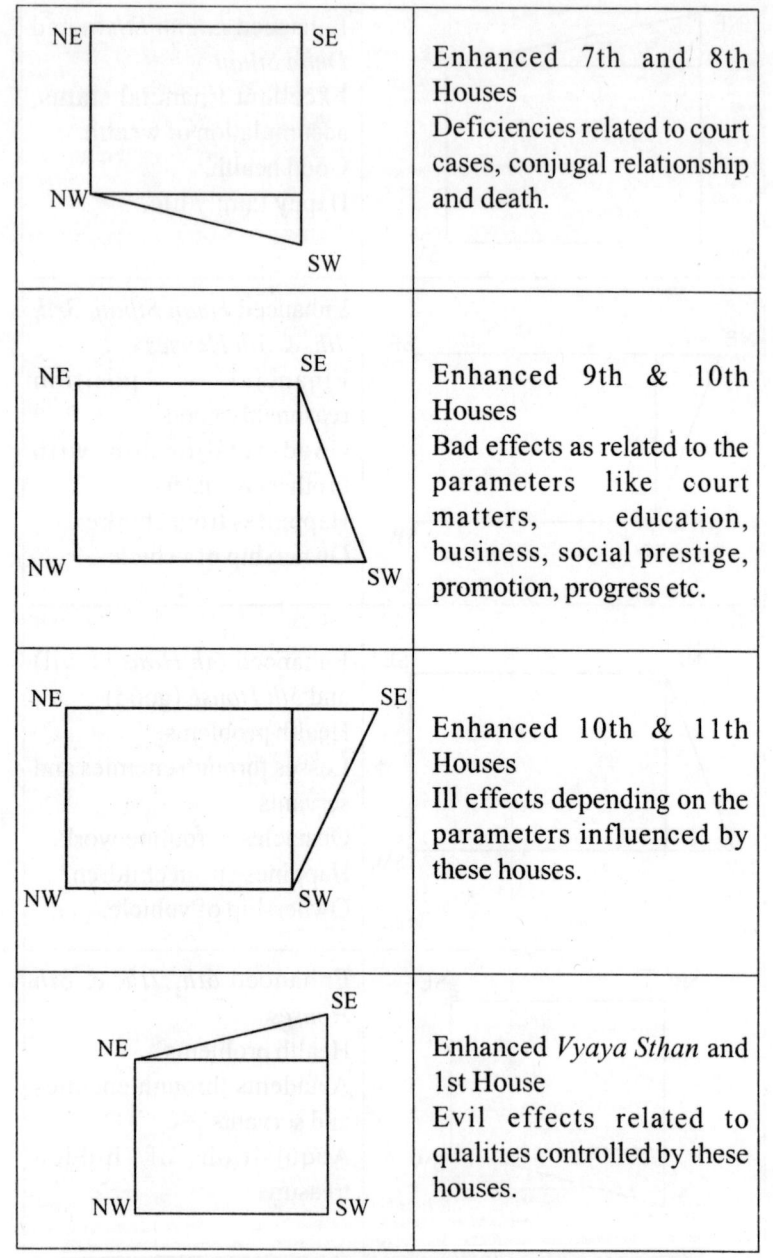

Shape	Significance
(plot with SW extension) NE, SE, NW, SW	**Enhanced 7th and 8th Houses** Deficiencies related to court cases, conjugal relationship and death.
(plot with SW extension) NE, SE, NW, SW	**Enhanced 9th & 10th Houses** Bad effects as related to the parameters like court matters, education, business, social prestige, promotion, progress etc.
(plot with SE extension) NE, SE, NW, SW	**Enhanced 10th & 11th Houses** Ill effects depending on the parameters influenced by these houses.
(plot with SE extension) NE, SE, NW, SW	**Enhanced *Vyaya Sthan* and 1st House** Evil effects related to qualities controlled by these houses.

Fig.17.3: Shape of a Plot and Astrological Significance (II)

Vastushastra Guidelines 167

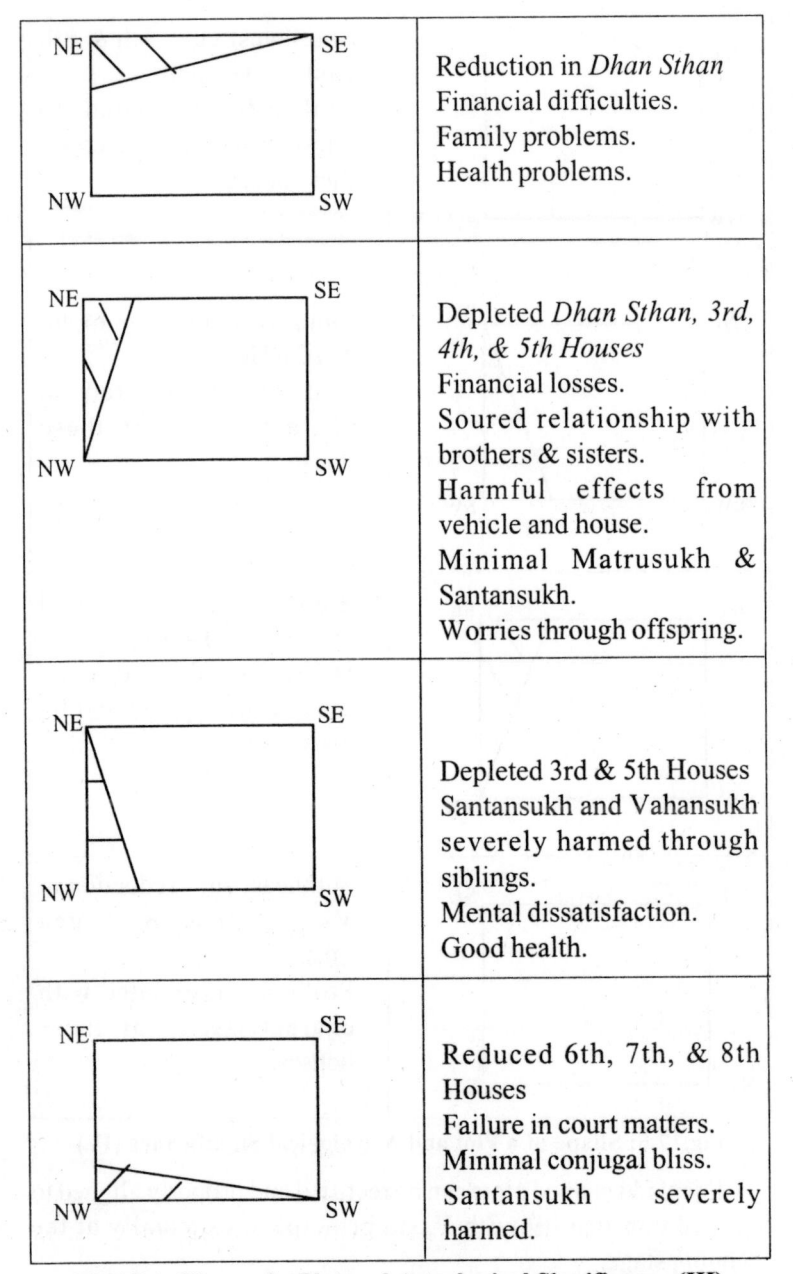

NE / SE / NW / SW (plot with NE cut diagonally)	Reduction in *Dhan Sthan* Financial difficulties. Family problems. Health problems.
NE / SE / NW / SW (plot with NW corner cut)	Depleted *Dhan Sthan, 3rd, 4th, & 5th Houses* Financial losses. Soured relationship with brothers & sisters. Harmful effects from vehicle and house. Minimal Matrusukh & Santansukh. Worries through offspring.
NE / SE / NW / SW (plot with west side slanted)	Depleted 3rd & 5th Houses Santansukh and Vahansukh severely harmed through siblings. Mental dissatisfaction. Good health.
NE / SE / NW / SW (plot with SW cut)	Reduced 6th, 7th, & 8th Houses Failure in court matters. Minimal conjugal bliss. Santansukh severely harmed.

Fig.17.4: Shape of a Plot and Astrological Significance (III)

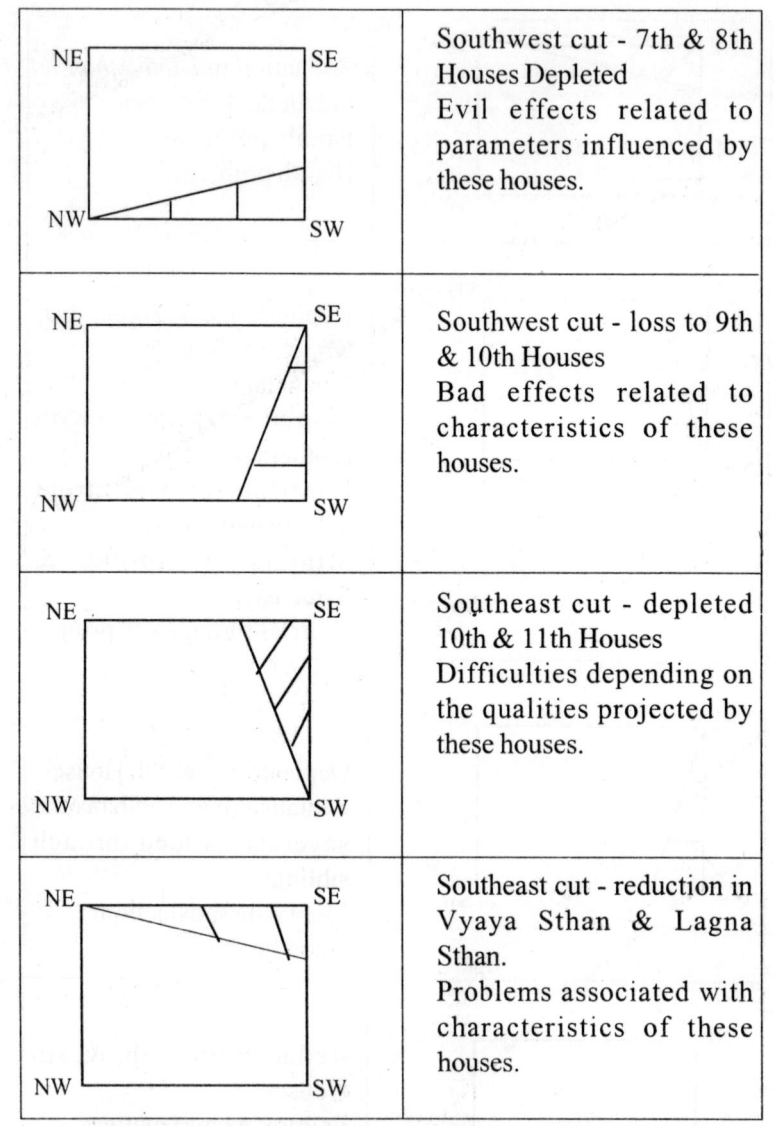

NE — SE / NW — SW (SW cut diagram)	Southwest cut - 7th & 8th Houses Depleted Evil effects related to parameters influenced by these houses.
NE — SE / NW — SW (SW cut diagram)	Southwest cut - loss to 9th & 10th Houses Bad effects related to characteristics of these houses.
NE — SE / NW — SW (SE cut diagram)	Southeast cut - depleted 10th & 11th Houses Difficulties depending on the qualities projected by these houses.
NE — SE / NW — SW (SE cut diagram)	Southeast cut - reduction in Vyaya Sthan & Lagna Sthan. Problems associated with characteristics of these houses.

Fig.17.5: Shape of a Plot and Astrological Significance (IV)

Even odd shaped plots can be rectified and properly aligned to achieve conformity with Vastu principles, especially at the planning stage.

17.3 Vithi Shula (Road Dead-end or Obstacle)

Good or bad effects due to single approach road to the plot depend on the zone in which the roads are located.

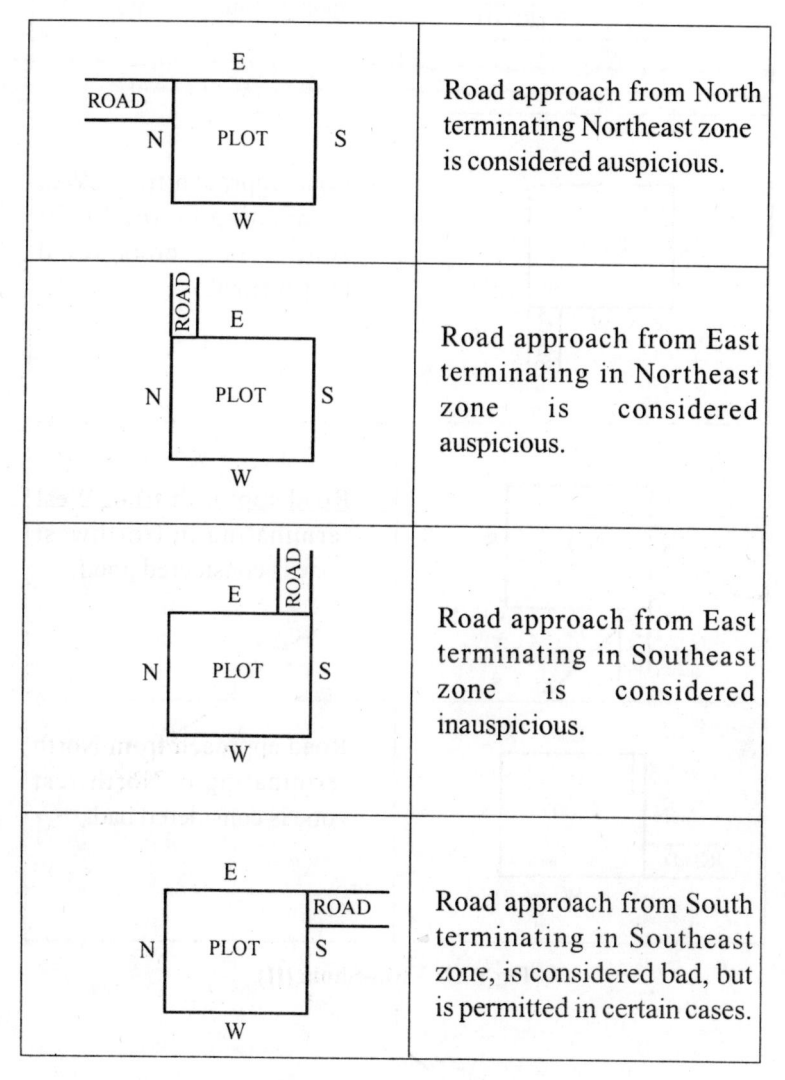

Diagram	Description
Road approaching from the North side, terminating at the Northeast zone of the plot.	Road approach from North terminating Northeast zone is considered auspicious.
Road approaching from the East side (top), terminating at the Northeast zone of the plot.	Road approach from East terminating in Northeast zone is considered auspicious.
Road approaching from the East side (top), terminating at the Southeast zone of the plot.	Road approach from East terminating in Southeast zone is considered inauspicious.
Road approaching from the South side, terminating at the Southeast zone of the plot.	Road approach from South terminating in Southeast zone, is considered bad, but is permitted in certain cases.

Fig.17.6: Vithi-Shula (I)

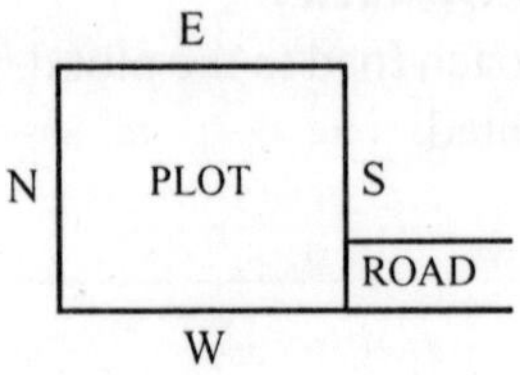	Road approach from South terminating in Southwest zone is considered inauspicious.
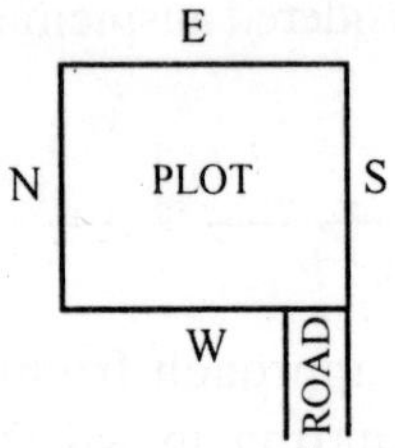	Road approach from West terminating in Southwest zone is considered inauspicious.
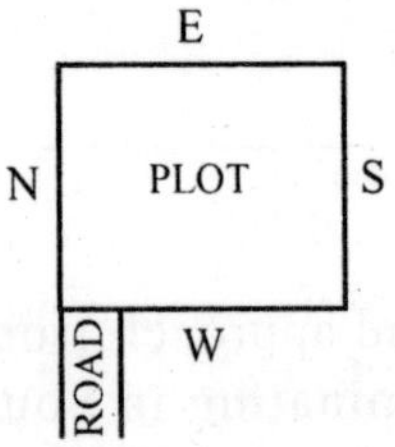	Road approach from West terminating in Northwest zone is considered good.
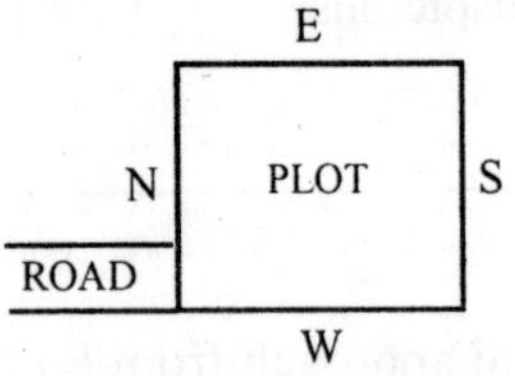	Road approach from North terminating in Northwest zone is considered bad.

Fig.17.7: Vithi-Shula (II)

Vastushastra Guidelines

In above charts, we have considered single approach roads for *Vithi-Shula* purposes. We can have plots with roads on two sides, three sides, or four sides. A plot having adjacent roads on South and West sides is considered good for trade and industry. Similarly, a plot with adjacent roads on North and West sides proves beneficial for the owner. A plot with roads on its three sides has its own advantages, while a plot having roads on all its four sides is perceived as auspicious.

Road Positioning	Projected Qualities
North and East	All types of benefits
North and West	Prosperity, achievements
East and South	Prosperity, satisfaction
East and West	Good if entrance from East
South and West	Average affluence
South and North	Affluence if entry from North
North, East, West	Progress and prosperity
East, North, South	Advancement in life
South, West, East	Good for trade and business
West, North, South	Expansion and growth

Benefits or virtues experienced by owners of such plots vary according to relative strength of directional virtues compared to any *Vastu-dosha* that may be observed. The above table gives brief outline of effects expected with regard to location of roads adjacent to a plot.

17.4 Vastu Rules for Agriculture
* Agricultural land should be divided into equal rectangular plots, preferably with breadth to length ratio of 1:1.618. The longer side should be oriented along the North-South axis, while the shorter side along the East-West direction.
* Electrical power points should be located in the Southeast corner.

- The bunds on the South and West sides should be at a higher level, while those on the East and North sides at a lower level or the ground on these sides should be a flat terrain.
- One-tenth of the plot on the Southwest side should be raised by constructing a solid stone parapet.
- The ground should have descending slopes towards the North and East sides.
- Trees should be planted in the South and West directions.
- Planting of trees in the North and East directions should be avoided.
- A well should be dug in the Northeast, North or East side of the plot.
- Any shed or a farmhouse on the plot should be constructed in the Southwest corner of the plot.

The following tenets of *Vastushastra* govern the landscaping process;

1. Making the Southwest side massive and heavy.
2. Loading the South direction.
3. Providing descending slopes towards the North, East and Northeast directions.
4. Constructing an underground water tank in the North, East or Northeast direction and providing a small water pond or open water body in one of these directions.
5. Elevating the compound walls on the South, Southwest and West directions and ensuring that these are massive and heavy.
6. Constructing the compound walls on the East, Northeast and North sides with light-weight material and maintaining these at a relatively lower elevation.
7. Locating the electrical power transformer and other electrical power points in the Southeast corner.
8. Constructing a cottage in the Southwest corner of the plot, with minimum side margins.
9. Planting of *Nilgiri* (eucalyptus) trees in the West zone of the plot, along with some varieties of medicinal, herbal and aromatic bushes.

The above tenets allow certain qualitative improvement in a *Vastu*, endowing it with virtues and purity. Few of the predominant effects are;
* Interrupting the South '*Pingala*' current flow.
* Achieving energy-mass balance through proportionate compensation for geomagnetic and energy disturbances.
* Augmenting the North '*Ida*' current flow, bestowing the Vastu with divine bliss.
* Regulating the excessive southern zone temperatures through water - vapour emission processes of trees like *Nilgiri* (eucalyptus) and *Neem* (margosa).
* Creating a healthy and salubrious atmosphere inside the house through scent and aroma of herbal plants.
* Enhancing the quality of the *Vastu* through beneficial effects of transverse polarisation of sunlight falling on an open water surface.

The rules or guidelines indicated here must be understood in a proper perspective and spirit. For successful application of rules, in-depth analysis and study must back up the whole exercise.

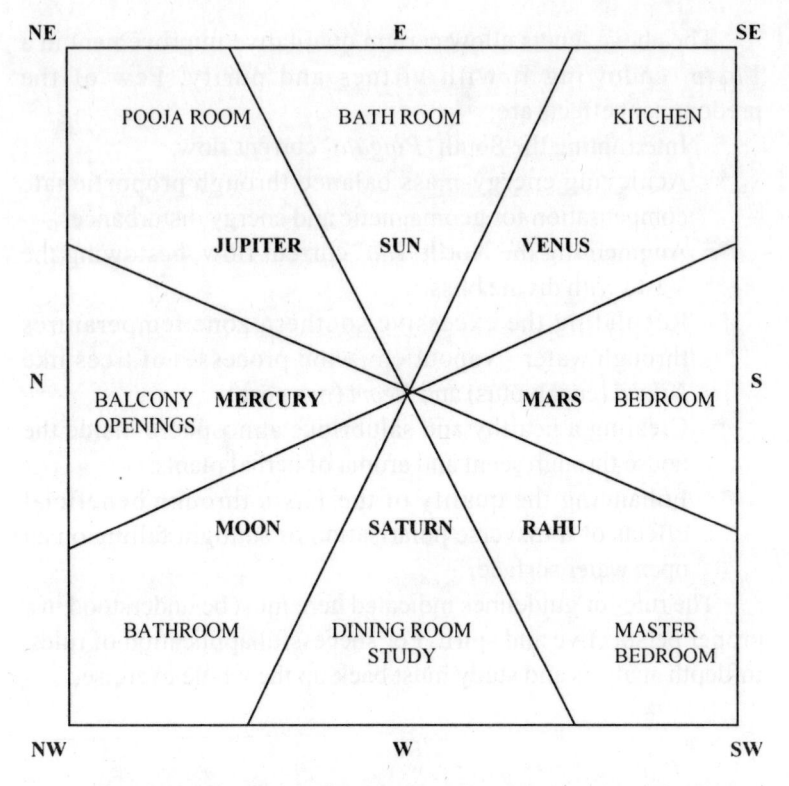

```
NE                    E                       SE
┌─────────────────────────────────────────────┐
│  POOJA ROOM    BATH ROOM      KITCHEN       │
│                                             │
│      JUPITER     SUN        VENUS           │
│                                             │
│  BALCONY  MERCURY           MARS  BEDROOM   │
│  OPENINGS                                   │
│                                             │
│       MOON      SATURN      RAHU            │
│                                             │
│   BATHROOM   DINING ROOM      MASTER        │
│              STUDY           BEDROOM        │
└─────────────────────────────────────────────┘
NW                    W                       SW
```

Fig.17.8: Planning of Rooms in a Household as per Vastu Principles

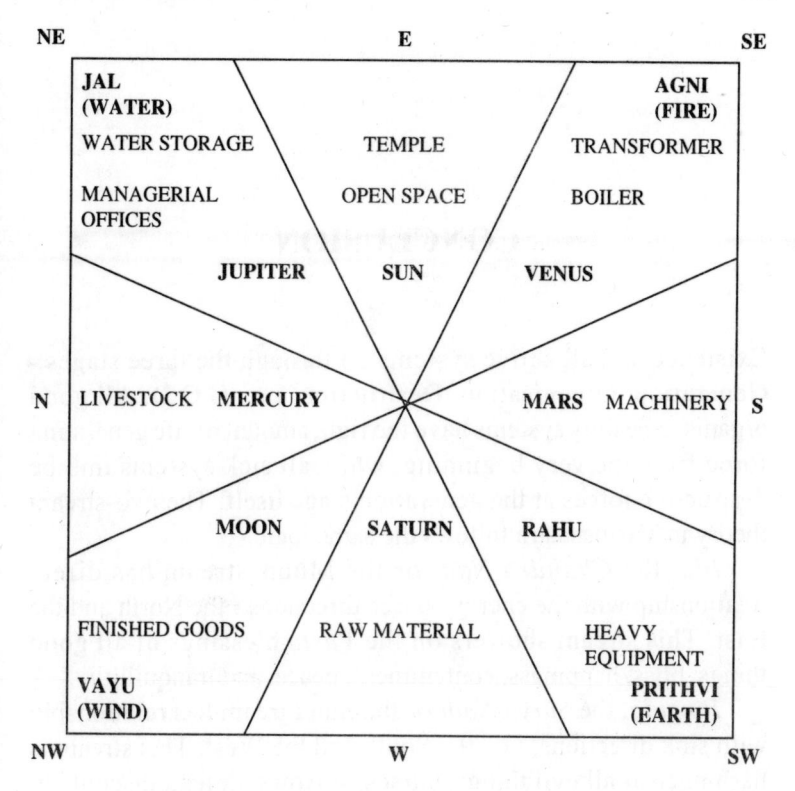

Fig.17.9: Industrial Layout as per Vastushastra

CONCLUSION

Existence and all active systems go through the three stages - Generation, Organisation, Destruction, i.e., G.O.D. All good organised healthy systems have the right amount of life generating force from the very beginning, while all sick systems imbibe destructive forces at the generation stage itself. The two-stream theory in Vastushastra follows the same logic.

Ida, the *Chandra Nadi* or the Moon Stream has direct relationship with the energy source directions - the North and the East. This stream showers on the *Vastu* blessings of all good things, bliss, happiness, contentment, peace, and tranquillity.

Pingala, the *Surya Nadi* or the Sun Stream has relationship with sink directions, i.e., the South and the West. This stream is harbinger of all evil things, curses, sorrows, defeat, discontent, grief, and torture.

* *Vastushastra* applications involve reinforcement of Ida, the Moon stream, and reduction of *Pingala* or the Sun stream.
* *Vastushastra* principles add the virtues of the source directions and subtract the vices of the sink directions.
* *Vastushastra* is technique for allowing free flow of energy from the North and the East directions, while blocking negative energies from the South and the West directions.
* *Vastushastra* is an art of developing a cosmic envelope around the *Vastu* that can provide rhythm, harmony, and tranquillity to the household.
* *Vastushastra* is an art of living with the natural flow of energy stream with all its creative virtues.
* *Vastushastra* is a science of controlling the event manifestation to open up a sky of possibilities and choices,

Conclusion

* *Vastushastra* is the will to live with a mysterious dimension that lies beyond the boundaries of conditioned reality and rationality.

This writing was directed towards understanding and interpreting the concepts from Astrology and *Yogashastra* from *Vastushastra* point of view. The general approach to the ancient sources of knowledge has become fragmentary in this era of specialisation. *Yogashastra*, Astrology, *Vastushastra*, *Ayurved*, and *Sangeet* are all sub-branches of *Darshanshastra*. But, over the years these sub-branches have evolved as separate disciplines and are studied as such.

There are experts in *Yogashastra* well versed in *Ayurved*, or experts in Astrology conversant with *Vastushastra*, or *Vastushastris* familiar with Sangeet and Astrology. But, an expert in all these disciplines is a rarity. This is unfortunate, since the key to ancient Indian knowledge about science lies in the logistics of *Darshanshastra*, and fragmentation of knowledge is depriving the present generation its rightful heritage and benefits thereof.

We have extensively covered significant areas of interest in *Yogashastra* and *Jyotisha*, which are essential in deciphering *Vastushastra* concepts. Various charts, tables, and *Vastu* rules illustrated in this book, together with tools from *Yogashastra* and Astrology can prove useful in comprehending core subjects in *Vastushastra*.

In the modern era, study of science has its own importance. Each and every discipline including Yoga is being subjected to scientific tests. There is nothing wrong in this exercise. But, the key issue here is, can the modern western science developed over last 300 years can be used as the only yardstick for assessing super sciences like *Vastushastra* formulated over 5000 years ago?

A time has come when a broader perspective is needed to study the ancient Indian sciences including Vastushastra. Establishing the correlation between *Vastushastra*, Astrology, and *Yogashastra* is just a small step in that direction. The authors only hope that this move will galvanise into a constructive movement to decipher the ancient scientific and logical knowledge.

178   *Mystic Science of Vastu*

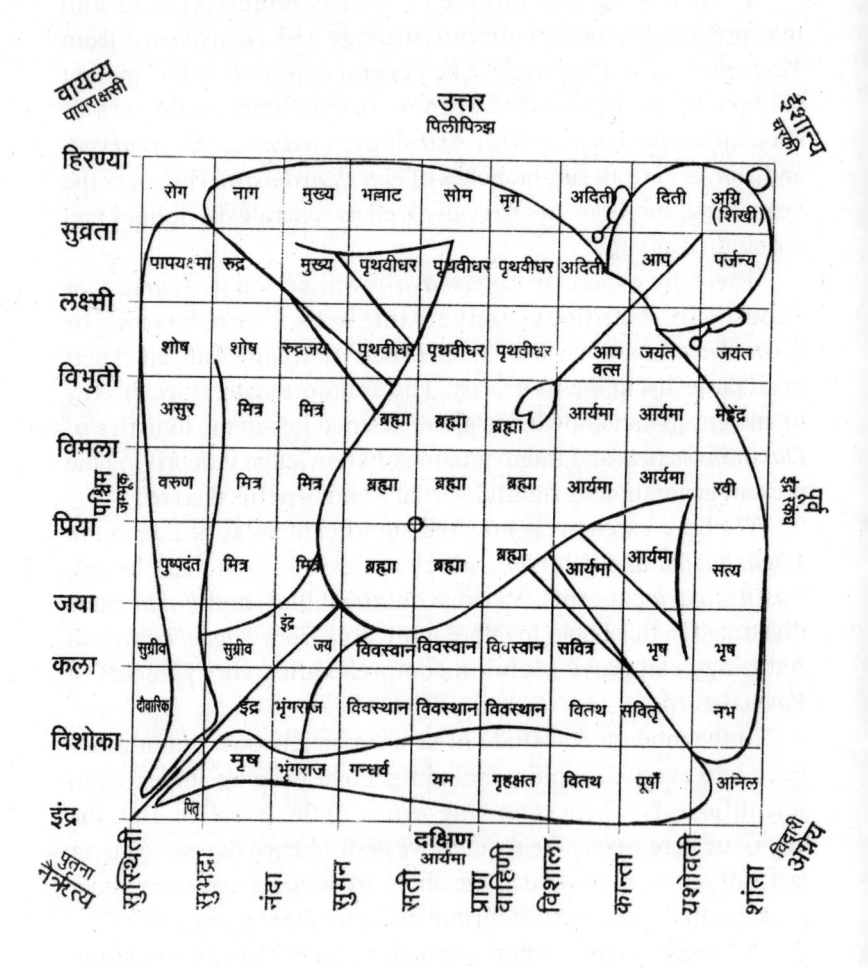

Conclusion

For advise, assistance, and consultation please contact:

1. Shri N. H. Sahasrabudhe
   Venkatesh Villa,
   1202/2A/1, Apte Road,
   Pune 411005 (India)
   Email: nhs@pn2.vsnl.net.in

2. Shri R. D. Mahatme
   P. O. Box 8129,
   Bandra East,
   Mumbai 400051 (India)
   Email: rdm@consultant.com

Information on Vastu Yantras and other Vastu related material indicated in this book is also available from;

Vastu Vidya Research Foundation
Pune 411005 (India)

Of Allied Interest

Secrets of Vastushastra
N.H. Sahasrabudh
R. D. Mahatme

Currently, a trend is evident wherein people are attempting Vastu changes by just referring to a couple of books on Vastushastra which follow a typical pattern — quoting some rules in Vastushastra and then presenting some success stories related to this analysis. But since the basic assumptions in formulation of these rules are not clearly defined, there is always a chance that rules may be misinterpreted and the application of these rules may not result in the desired solution. This book departs from this set pattern to analyse the logic behind Vastushastra in a unique manner by not only elucidating Vastushastra principles, but also laying due emphasis on the extensive study that must go into kind of Vastu analysis.

It seeks convergence between Yogashastra and Vastushastra, Astrology and Vastushastra, Modern Science and Vastushastra, etc. This approach has also been discussed in relation to practical problems. A novel concept of 'Balancing and Dynamic Planning' would prove useful for students in this field to understand the essence of Vastu concepts. It is not advisable to go in for reckless structural alternations in the pursuit of instant material gains. Vastushastra basically aims at peace of mind and a healthy life for the dweller, which requires a multidisciplinary approach while applying those principles.

ISBN 81 207 2042 3 Rs. 100